Sound, Scene & Story

Sound, Scene Story

An Introduction to Creative Writing

by Pat MacEnulty, Ph.D.

Second Edition

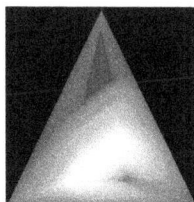

PRISM LIGHT
PRESS

ISBN 978-0-9898066-0-2

Published by
Prism Light Press
PO Box 625, Tallahassee, FL 32302
www.prismlightpress.com

Manufactured in the United States of America.

Table of Contents

Introduction

Introduction -- Read Me!

We live in the age of the image – still pictures on billboards, in magazines, and on online platforms such as Instagram; movies; TV shows; professional and amateur videos on YouTube, and so on. Who needs writing anymore? For one thing, writing is hard. It requires a knowledge of spelling and grammar rules. You need to constantly learn new words in order to be able to truly express your ideas. And it's time consuming to read and write.

Yet people continue to do both because reading and writing engage our imaginations in a way that the image alone, for all its wondrous properties, cannot do. Reading and writing force us to use our minds, creating order out of small lines and squiggles on paper or screen. These activities enable us to transmit our thoughts and feelings in a simple, direct manner and to understand the thoughts and feelings of others. When we read we are required to use our imaginations. When we write -- even more so. Using the imagination helps us develop problem-solving skills: we learn how to navigate in a complex world, and, most importantly, we connect with others. We realize we are not alone in the world.

We are often drawn to writing because we have an innate (or inborn) urge to play with language. Children make up silly rhymes, comedians make us laugh with the unexpected things they say, punsters make us groan, and rappers, poets and singers take us to joyful heights and painful depths through the skillful use of language. Writing, especially creative writing, allows us to explore the infinite possibilities inherent in words and word play.

Writing also gives us an outlet for sharing our stories. Human beings are compelled by stories. Stories thrill us; they frighten us; they make us laugh. They awaken something within us. We developed language so we could tell our stories to each other and so we could relate what was going on in our hearts and minds to our friends, families, and even strangers. We developed writing so we could communicate with one another on a wider level -- with those we know and with those we will never know.

The first writing was used as a means of recording laws and historical events, but eventually it was put to use creatively as a way to delve into the wide range of human experience from the horrors of war to the vagaries of love. This need has not gone away. We still need to understand what it means to be human, and we still want to express that meaning from our own unique perspective. Creative writing gives us the tools to do that.

The Purpose of This Book

This book is designed to be an introduction to three main genres of creative writing and to provide you with strategies for writing creatively in any field. You may wonder why anyone would need strategies for creative writing. As the newspaper columnist Red Smith is quoted as saying: "You simply sit down at the typewriter, open your veins, and bleed." (These days, we'd say you sit down with your computer, your tablet or even your phone, but the idea is the same: you pour out your heart and soul onto the page.) That sounds easy, but there's more to creative writing than simply expressing yourself.

Creative writing is both an art and a skill. To be any good at it takes practice, patience, and perseverance. It's like cooking. Anyone can pour a can of beans into a pan and heat them up. But to be a great chef, you must study, you must get in the kitchen as much as possible, and you must be adventurous and be willing to take risks.

This book provides an introduction to the processes that creative writers use whether they are writing poetry, drama, or prose narrative. You will find that it's useful to learn the rudiments of each of these genres as they are not as separate as they might seem. Each one informs and enhances the other. Good drama needs narrative. Good narrative relies on the adept use of language, and good poetry incorporates imagery, story, and ideas. Think of them as three roads that criss-cross each other, leading to the exact same place: the heart and mind of the reader or listener.

How to Use This Book

Although *Sound, Scene & Story* provides a useful introduction to the creative writing arts for anyone, it is specifically designed to be used in an educational or workshop setting and therefore contains assignments and blank pages for writing. I encourage you to write in this book: doodle, write poems and comments in the margins as well as on the blank pages; make it your own.

You will keep a blog for this course either in a school blog or using a platform such as Wordpress. You will find blog assignments at the end of the chapters as well as homework assignments, which should be turned into your instructor or shared with the class. If you prefer, you may use a hand written journal rather than a blog. If you are not in an educational setting, you may want to do the work in the book with a partner or a writing group. In addition to writing your own blogs, you should make a habit of reading the blogs of your peers and responding to them in the comments area.

Each chapter ends with examples of student writing that are pertinent to the material in that chapter. The samples come from both high school and college students. They are often responses to exercises and may not have had the benefit of revision. The reason for this is to emphasize the process aspect of writing. Your writing doesn't have to come out perfect the first time. You might never "perfect" it, but you'll never even get close if you don't take that first step of getting out of your head and onto a page.

The sample writing pages are followed by a short vocabulary assignment. The words will be either creative writing terms or words from the readings that may be unfamiliar to you. You should fill in the definitions in your own words and/or include an example of the term used correctly. At some point you should start finding vocabulary words on your own from reading or discussions. Building your vocabulary is a life-long process, so you may as well get in the habit now.

Finally, there are several writing prompts after the vocabulary. If you are in a class or working with a writing group, you may want to respond to the prompts together and then share your writing with the class or group. Or you may do them on your own. These writings should not be judged or critiqued. Rather, think of them as warm-up exercises. Setting a ten-minute limit will help you circumvent writer's block. No one can be expected to write a perfect piece of writing in ten minutes. So it's important not to apologize or explain your responses to the prompts.

In my experience, writers are often surprised by what comes out in these writing exercises. By directly accessing the unconscious, we sometimes find buried treasure. Sometimes a piece will come out exactly the way you want it to. Other times, there may be one sentence that sparks an entire story or poem later on. And sometimes, it's just a way of clearing out the clutter in your brain. Remember, no judgment!

If you are in an educational setting, you may be asked to type selected writings and post them to your blog. Your class may produce a separate blog or print publication to feature the best work of the class so you should label and carefully edit the pieces that you want to be reprinted or published on the blog.

Blog/Journal Assignment:

For your first blog post or journal entry, write a summary of your experiences with creative writing. What do you like to write? What do you like to read? What's your favorite type of creative writing?

Chapter One
What Does It Mean to be a Creative Writer?

Creative writing is about you: your thoughts, dreams, fantasies, feelings, and ideas. It is an expression of that which is inside your heart and your mind. Creative writing is also about connecting with readers and bringing them into the world(s) you have created.

Sometimes students think that creative writing has fewer rules than expository writing, but that isn't necessarily the case. It's just that the rules are more flexible, and writers are often deemed more original when they break the rules. What beginning writers often don't realize is that great writers know the rules thoroughly before they break them.

In this book, you'll be introduced to some rules, but I urge you to think of them more as guidelines. These guidelines aren't arbitrary. They are there to make the communication of your thoughts and feelings more effective and thereby make writing a more rewarding experience for you, and reading a more rewarding experience for your readers.

What makes it creative?

You've read a lot of different types of writing in your life. You've probably read textbooks, Facebook profiles, recipes, directions to a friend's house, text messages from friends, and emails as well as short stories, poems and novels.

The kind of writing you find in a textbook or an instruction manual is called "expository." It means that the writer tries to be objective and informative. It is meant to help the reader do something, learn something, or understand something. It is generally not meant to create an emotional response in the reader.

Creative writing, on the other hand, is subjective and evokes an emotional response. The events and experiences described are filtered through one or more points of view. Creative writing establishes a connection between the reader and the writer at the feeling level. Creative writing may create a mood as in an Edgar Allan Poe story. Or it may be designed to entertain you and make you forget about your problems for a while; millions of people have found themselves swept away by the stories in the Harry Potter books and *The Hunger Games* trilogy. Like expository writing, creative writing can be informative. In fact, it often is. But it is never reducible to "pure information." It is also about making the reader feel something, and often encourages a reader to think critically and theoretically about the "information" contained in the text.

Genre

The word genre means type or kind. So when we speak of genres of writing, we are talking about the different kinds of creative writing:

- poetry
- drama
- narrative prose (fiction or creative non-fiction)

These categories can be further divided. For instance, fiction can mean science fiction, romance, detective fiction, horror or literary fiction. [Here's where it gets really confusing: when someone refers to "genre fiction," that person is talking specifically about science fiction/fantasy, romance, horror or detective fiction. This is to differentiate between fiction that adheres to a particular set of narrative conventions and literary fiction, which typically does not adhere to a particular formula or set of conventions.]

In this course we will examine each of the above genres – poetry, drama and narrative prose. And we'll specifically look at the main quality of each: sound for poetry, scene for drama, and story for narrative prose. Remember, however, that poems can also contain stories; sound is important in both drama and narrative prose; and narrative prose usually has scenes, while the scenes in a dramatic piece would be meaningless without a story. This interconnectivity explains why it is helpful for any writer to become fluent in all three elements: sound, scene, and story.

Writers Read

Emily Dickinson wrote:

> There is no Frigate like a Book
> To take us Lands away,
> Nor any Coursers like a Page
> Of prancing Poetry –
> This Traverse may the poorest take
> Without oppress of Toll –
> How frugal is the Chariot
> That bears a Human soul.

The best way to learn how to write is to read. All great writers are great readers. They read the works of the ancients, and they read the works of their contemporaries. They read not just for pleasure or information, but also in order to study and sometimes absorb the techniques of other writers.

Reading gives you a feel for the way language works, it broadens your vocabulary, and it helps you understand the underlying structures that writers use. As you read and are exposed to the styles of other writers, you will slowly start to develop your own style. The other advantage of being a voracious reader is that you learn more about the world, about history, and about the inner workings of the human mind and the human heart. This knowledge helps you to develop wisdom and insight -- good qualities for a writer to have.

Reading keeps writers involved in a conversation with thinkers around the world and throughout time. Reading the stories that others have written often inspires writers to take that story and make it their own. A few years back there was a movie called *Clueless*. This movie is actually a retelling of a story written 200 years ago by Jane Austen -- the story of *Emma*.

Writers learn how to write by reading, they get ideas by reading, and they join in the larger conversation of the world by reading. In addition to reading books, today's writers read newspapers, magazines, and Internet publications. They often try to keep up with plays, movies and TV shows. Some of them are politically active. Some of them travel in search of interesting settings. Writers are not off living in some ivory tower. Writers are involved with the most important issues of the day, and that's often what they write about.

Process

Typically, the first question any writer is asked is "What is your process?" People want to know the following:

- Do you write all day or only at a certain time of day?
- Do you use a pen and paper or write directly onto the computer?
- Do you write an outline first or do you just start writing?
- Do you do a lot of research or make everything up?
- Are you slow and methodical or do you write fast and flesh it out later?

The answers to these questions are different for every writer. Some writers go to coffee shops to write. Some writers get up at 5 a.m. every day to write. Some writers think about their story or poem for a long time until they have it set in their heads. Just as process changes from one writer to another, it can also change for one writer over the course of time. To find out the right process for you, you should experiment with a few different methods.

Your Idea Bank

Where do writers get their ideas? Even they can't always tell you. In Ancient Greece, many people believed that creativity was a gift from the gods. Among the Greek gods and goddesses, there are nine sisters known as the muses. The muses are the daughters of Zeus and Mnemosyne (Memory). Each muse has her own area of expertise. For example, Calliope is the muse for epic poetry; Erato (think of the word "erotic") is the muse for love poetry. History, comedy, and tragedy each have their own muses.

Writers still speak of "the muse" -- that creative spark that ignites the imagination. They complain about being ignored by the muse. They try to find their muse. They try to summon the muse. They write love poems to the muse. The muse is the personification of the creative process. And that process begins with ideas.

Writers may say they get their ideas from the muse, but writers are always on the lookout for ideas either consciously or unconsciously. One way to begin collecting ideas is to keep an idea journal. This is not necessarily a diary although you may wish to record the bits and pieces of your life in it if you choose.

Your idea journal is where you:

- Ask questions
- Write down descriptions
- Pour out your feelings
- Let your mind play

Many writers would not go anywhere without a journal. You never know when the muse is going to hit you over the head with an idea. Some writers advise journaling each morning. Julia Cameron, author of *The Artist's Way*, advocates writing three pages every day in long hand: "The morning pages are three pages of stream-of-consciousness longhand morning writing. You should think of them not as 'art' but as an active form of meditation for Westerners. In the morning pages we declare to the world—and ourselves—what we like, what we dislike, what we wish, what we hope, what we regret, and what we plan."

Creative Play and Rituals

When you are courting the muse, you are letting the creative part of your mind know that you are interested in what it has to tell you. Often we may have an idea, but immediately we think: "that's stupid, who cares about that?" or "I don't have time." That's the left part of your brain talking. The left hemisphere of the brain is the logical part of the brain and also the critical part of the brain. Part of being a creative writer is allowing the right brain, the side that is more illogical and more creative, to express itself.

Left Brain	Right Brain
logical	emotional
mathematical	visual
verbal	symbolic
detail oriented	looks at big picture
reality based	fantasy based
forms strategies	looks at possibilities
practical	impetuous
safe	risky

How do we activate and engage the creative side of the brain? Here are three methods:

- Free writing: Write as much as you can without stopping for a set time period, say five to ten minutes. Don't edit, don't worry about spelling or grammar or how it sounds. Don't worry about making sense. Sometimes the creative part of your mind doesn't make sense. Afterwards you can go back and underline sentences, phrases, or words that seem interesting. Then you can free write or cluster around those ideas. When you cluster, you allow your mind to work in a nonlinear manner. After you've done a free write and/or a cluster, then you can bring in the left brain to help you create a story or poem.

- Another method is to play. Children never suffer from "play block." Try finger painting or creating with clay, spend time with young children, go to a playground and act like a little kid. You could also take an improv class where you'll learn all kinds of games that will help spark your creativity.

- The third method is to try writing or drawing with your non-dominant hand. In other words, if you are right-handed, write or draw with your left hand. If you are left-handed, try writing or drawing with your right hand. For instance, you might take a crayon with your left hand (if you are right handed) and just let the crayon flow into some kind of design. Then with your right hand create something more logical out of the design made by your left hand. Writing for even a page of two with your non-dominant hand will help fire the neurons in the creative half of your brain.

Writing Rituals

Writing rituals signal to your brain that it is time to get in the creative mode. In establishing writing rituals, writers look at the following elements of their process:

- Location – Some writers like to go outside with a notebook and sit outside in nature or in a public place to write. Others need to write in the solitude of their bedroom or office. Still others like to write in coffee shops. And some writers do any of the above depending on how they feel that day.
- Time – Establishing certain times of the day for writing helps us get in the writing habit. When writing becomes a habit, it has become an established part of your life.
- Behavior – We all have little things that help quiet our mind. When our mind is full of worry and distraction, it's difficult to concentrate on something creative. So having a quiet mind is important. Sometimes it means straightening up the area where we are about to work. Or it may mean having a cup of coffee or tea before we start to work. Spending a few minutes quietly with eyes closed, breathing deeply will help quiet the mind as well.

What Do You Know?

There's an old piece of advice that has been given to writers, probably since the days of Homer: write what you know. Now, you may think that what you know is boring and wouldn't be of any interest to anyone else. What you may not realize is that you are the only person in the entire universe who knows exactly what you know. You are unique. And because we are infinitely curious as human beings, others will be interested in what you know -- and in your own particular way of looking at the world.

So what are the things you know about?

- your family
- your friends
- your school
- your childhood
- your religious practices
- your games
- your favorite things: food, music, etc.
- your dreams and aspirations

All of these things have provided rich fodder for writers over the centuries.

Writing what you know doesn't mean that you can only write about places you have been and experiences you have personally had. If that was the case, J.K. Rowling could never have written the Harry Potter books, J.R.R. Tolkien could never have created The *Lord of the Rings*, and Lewis Carroll certainly never would have let Alice fall down the rabbit hole into Wonderland.

What those writers did was take what they knew (human dreams, emotions and aspirations) and then used their imaginations to create a new world where these familiar ideas could have new life.

Hogwarts is similar in many ways to an English boarding school. The Hobbits have human qualities. And while there was no white rabbit with a pocket watch, there actually was a real Alice, who inspired *Alice in Wonderland*.

Writers make a point of increasing what they know by doing research. They talk to people, they travel if they can, they take classes in history and science, and, of course, they read.

The point of writing what you know is that if you grow up in a tropical area and have never seen or felt snow in your life, your descriptions of a balmy night in paradise are probably going to be more accurate than your description of a blizzard in North Dakota. For writers just starting out, writing about the subjects that are closest to home usually is the best way to learn the craft of writing, but remember: writing what you know is not just an admonition to be confident in what is familiar, it is also a rallying cry to learn more every day. For instance, in the situation above, if you live in the tropics and want to write about snow, you should go somewhere and experience it.

Your First Tool for Writing: Words

Writers love words. They collect words the way other people collect comic books or baseball cards. Without words you simply can't express all the thoughts and feelings that you have.

When a writer comes across a word she doesn't know, she looks it up in the dictionary. Then she tries to use the word when the situation calls for it. A dictionary gives the literal meaning of a word, the archaic meaning of a word, and sometimes the root meaning of the word -- which can be fascinating in itself. Online dictionaries provide a recording of the correction pronunciation. Some dictionaries also give examples of the word in use. Word lovers have been known to peruse dictionaries in search of interesting words.

Choosing the right word

Whether we are writing creative or expository writing, word choice is critical. Creative writers pay close attention to the connotative meaning as well as the denotative meaning of words to make sure they express the right thoughts and feelings.

Consider this pair of words: residence & home.

Both words refer to a dwelling place, a place where people live. The denotation or "dictionary definition" is quite similar. Compare the dictionary.com definitions of the words:

- home: "house, apartment, or other shelter that is the usual residence of a person, family, or household."
- residence: "the place, esp. the house, in which a person lives or resides; dwelling place; home"

These two words are so similar in meaning that they are used in the definitions of each other. But each word has a different connotation. Home has a warm feeling to it. It makes people think of comfort and family. Residence is a much more clinical word. It may have a feeling of temporariness. It certainly doesn't evoke a sense of comfort.

Writers also try to avoid phrases that have grown stale with use. An old literary joke makes fun of the book that begins, "It was a dark and stormy night." This phrase has become a cliché, a joke about bad writing. If you want to connect with readers, you need to stimulate their imaginations with fresh ways of seeing the world.

Another aspect of word choice involves differentiating between concrete and abstract words. Writers like to "show" through concrete terms, although sometimes we have to "tell" through abstract terms. Concrete words apply to physical things such as rocks, tables, houses, sunsets. Abstract words apply to ideas, such as happy, nice, painful, disgusting.

As you read, study, and play with language, you will be able to use connotation and denotation to your advantage, you will be able to identify a cliché, and you will understand the difference between concrete and abstract terms. These skills will strengthen your writing.

Avoiding wordiness

While writers like to have lots of different words at their disposal, they also know that too many words (especially unnecessary words) can clutter up a good piece of writing and cause readers to lose interest. An essential part of the rewriting process, which we'll discuss at the end of the book, is going through and deleting superfluous words. Minimalist writers such as Hemingway taught us that we can often say more with less.

If you haven't read Hemingway, try starting off with his short story, "Hills Like White Elephants" which you can easily find on the Internet. Notice how spare the descriptions are. There isn't much action, and the dialogue is cryptic, meaning you're not sure what the characters are really saying. But if you read it a couple of times and realize what the story is actually about, then suddenly everything makes sense. Although it is a short story where nothing much happens, the stakes are actually quite high!

Journaling

A blog is a great place to write your ideas and assignments, but many writers swear by hand writing in a journal as a way to foster creativity. Blogs are usually public, but a private journal can house your innermost secrets. I encourage you to do both. If you don't already have a journal, go out and buy one. It can be a fancy leather-bound or moleskin book that you buy from a bookstore or gift shop or it can be as simple as a composition or sketch book. Make a commitment to write in it every morning. You might record your dreams, you might write down descriptions, or you might write down your private thoughts. Read your journal regularly to find ideas for your creative writing. In those pages you'll find the seeds for stories, poems and plays.

Blog/Journal assignments:

1. Make a list of your favorite books as well as any magazines, newspapers, and blogs that you like to read. Choose one and discuss.

2. Think about the process you will use for this class (or the one you will start out using) and answer the following questions:

- What time of day will you write?
- Will you write in longhand first or directly onto the computer?
- Do you want to use prompts to get started?
- Do you have any rituals like sharpening pencils or drinking a special cup of coffee or tea before getting started?

Reading Assignment:

Look up the story "Hills Like White Elephants" by Ernest Hemmingway and read it. Write a one-paragraph reaction to the story. If you don't understand what the story is about, read some of the criticism about it.

Student Writing Sample

This piece of writing comes from an exercise I do in class that I call "Confessional Booth." First, the writers identify five to ten different selves (angry self, happy self, little kid self, party self, etc.). Then for ten minutes, they write in the voice of that particular self. This is a great exercise for writing what you know, for whom do we know better than ourselves? Remember, the following is just an exercise, not a finished piece of writing.

Alone Self

I feel alone. Better yet I am alone. As alone as I can be. A million faces surround me day and night. Laughter is spread amongst us, yet I am alone. I feel as if my real self can never touch the surface. As if I have to hide everything I feel and believe because I have not one person that will say "I agree," or "that's how I feel." Alone is how everyone feels inside, but I'm not everyone. I can relate to no one. Yet why do I always need someone with me? The times I want to be alone, I can't. In my mind friends are people who shouldn't make you feel alone. Yet I have not met anyone I can actually be alone with.

-- Jessica Dianna Neal

Vocabulary

Define the following and add any new words that you have encountered recently:

Archaic

Cliché

Connotation

Denotation

Evoke

Expository

Formulaic

Genre

Objective

Stream-of-consciousness

Subjective

Writing Prompts

1. Make a list of 15-20 words that you like and then write a 250-word passage using as many as you can.

2. Write what you know! Describe your best friend: appearance, dress, mannerisms, typical things he or she says, a funny thing he or she did.

3. 3. Make a list of five to ten of the selves that live inside you. Write a "confession" or an explanation from the point of view of one of your different selves.

Unit One

Sound

Chapter Two
Poetry: What to Know Before You Go

"Poetry is language that sounds better and means more."
- Charles Wright
Quarter Notes, 1995

For this first section when we are examining the role of sound in creative writing, we will focus on poetry. Of course, poetry is also dependent on imagery, figures of speech, and themes, but it is the way the words fall on the ear that ultimately matters in poetry.

What is Poetry?

There are many different definitions for poetry. In general, we might say that poetry is an arrangement of carefully chosen words that expresses a thought or feeling and conveys a meaning. But that definition can cover a lot of ground so let's try to describe what we mean by poetry.

Traditional poems are easy to spot. They rhyme and have a distinct meter. They may be broken up into stanzas (groups of related lines similar to a paragraph in prose writing), and the lines may be approximately the same length. When you look at this piece of writing by the great romantic poet William Wordsworth, you have no doubt that you are looking at a poem:

I Wandered Lonely as a Cloud

by William Wordsworth

I wandered lonely as a cloud
  That floats on high o'er vales and hills,
When all at once I saw a crowd,
  A host, of golden daffodils;
Beside the lake, beneath the trees,
Fluttering and dancing in the breeze.

Continuous as the stars that shine
  And twinkle on the Milky Way,
They stretched in never-ending line

Along the margin of a bay:
Ten thousand saw I at a glance,
Tossing their heads in sprightly dance.

The waves beside them danced, but they
  Out-did the sparkling waves in glee:
A Poet could not but be gay,
  In such a jocund company:
I gazed--and gazed--but little thought
What wealth the show to me had brought:

For oft, when on my couch I lie
  In vacant or in pensive mood,
They flash upon that inward eye
  Which is the bliss of solitude;
And then my heart with pleasure fills,
And dances with the daffodils.

Poetry is a natural way to express feelings and tell stories. That's the reason for its enduring popularity from the oral tradition of early Africans and Ancient Greeks to the performance poets on stages around America. Poetry is our 'go-to' outlet for our passions.

Following are a few poetic definitions by poets themselves:

Poetry is like fingerprints
on a window, behind which
A child who can't sleep
stands waiting for dawn.
    -- Herman de Coninck, The Plural of Happiness, 2006

A poem is a cup of words open to the sky and wind in a bucket.
    -- Naomi Shihab Nye, The Poetry Paper, no. 3, 2006

Poetry is like standing on the edge of a lake on a moonlit night and the light of the moon is always pointing straight at you.
    -- Billy Collins, Portsmouth Herald, 23 January 2005

Write your own definition of poetry here: _____

_____

_____

_____

Now that we've considered what poetry is, let's think about what we expect a poem to do. Here are some ideas.

A poem should:

- say something meaningful
- express or evoke a feeling
- be pleasing in its form

Understanding Poetry

Writing poetry is an act of discovery. It means going into uncharted territory, journeying where no one has gone before because each poem is a unique expression of the particular experience of a particular person in a particular place and time. Reading poetry is also an act of discovery.

In order to write poetry, you should read all kinds of poetry and start working toward understanding it. Poetry rarely comes at its meaning head-on. Rather it approaches truth at an angle or, as Emily Dickinson says, "tell[s] the truth but tell[s] it slant." Therefore understanding poetry may require that we study it and analyze it by breaking it down into different parts. Don't be dismayed if you don't understand a poem on the first read. Sometimes uncovering the meaning is the most rewarding part.

Following are some different aspects of poetry:

- Speaker and Audience -- Every poem must have a speaker and an audience. The poem may be written in the first person (I or we), the second person (you), the third person (he, she, or they), or using an omniscient speaker. But there is always a speaker. The speaker may be the poet or it may be a persona that the poet adopts. As for audience, sometimes the poet is writing to a specific "you" in the poem. Other poems may be directed toward the general reader.
- Subject and Theme -- A poem must also have a subject. It must be about something. Poems are often about the larger aspects of life: love, death, childbirth, heartbreak, growing old, nature, the self, or historical events. Or sometimes a poem might be about something apparently quite small, like a bee.
- Tone -- The poet's attitude toward the subject of the poem is conveyed by the tone of the poem. Tone most often is conveyed by diction, or word choice. But it is also

conveyed by the imagery, figures of speech and sound of the poem. (We will cover these aspects in future chapters.) Tone is directly related to the parts of the poem. It is used to create the mood of the poem.

Here are some steps for understanding poetry:

- Read the title. What do you expect the poem to be about?
- Identify the poem's speaker and the intended audience.
- Ask yourself what the poem is about on the literal level before trying to figure out what it might mean on a symbolic level.
- When was the poem written? Will researching the context of the poem help you understand it? What personal information about the poet will help you understand it? For instance, if you know that Sylvia Plath's father died when she was young and that she battled depression for most of her life, you will be able to better understand many of her darker motifs and themes.
- THIS IS KEY: Look up any words you don't understand. You cannot understand a poem if you do not know the meaning of the words. In a poem, every word is key.
- Talk to your peers about the poem. Listen to their interpretations and insights.

Read the first eight stanzas of "The Raven" by Edgar Allan Poe.

Once upon a midnight dreary, while I pondered, weak and weary,
Over many a quaint and curious volume of forgotten lore,
While I nodded, nearly napping, suddenly there came a tapping,
As of someone gently rapping, rapping at my chamber door.
" 'Tis some visitor," I muttered, "tapping at my chamber door;
Only this, and nothing more."

Ah, distinctly I remember, it was in the bleak December,
And each separate dying ember wrought its ghost upon the floor.
Eagerly I wished the morrow; vainly I had sought to borrow
From my books surcease of sorrow, sorrow for the lost Lenore,
For the rare and radiant maiden whom the angels name Lenore,
Nameless here forevermore.

And the silken sad uncertain rustling of each purple curtain
Thrilled me---filled me with fantastic terrors never felt before;
So that now, to still the beating of my heart, I stood repeating,
"'Tis some visitor entreating entrance at my chamber door,

Some late visitor entreating entrance at my chamber door.
This it is, and nothing more."

Presently my soul grew stronger; hesitating then no longer,
"Sir," said I, "or madam, truly your forgiveness I implore;
But the fact is, I was napping, and so gently you came rapping,
And so faintly you came tapping, tapping at my chamber door,
That I scarce was sure I heard you." Here I opened wide the door;---
Darkness there, and nothing more.

Deep into that darkness peering, long I stood there wondering, fearing,
Doubting, dreaming dreams no mortal ever dared to dream before;
But the silence was unbroken, and the darkness gave no token,
And the only word there spoken was the whispered word, `Lenore!'
This I whispered, and an echo murmured back the word, `Lenore!'
Merely this and nothing more.

Back into the chamber turning, all my soul within me burning,
Soon again I heard a tapping somewhat louder than before.
`Surely,' said I, `surely that is something at my window lattice;
Let me see then, what thereat is, and this mystery explore -
Let my heart be still a moment and this mystery explore; -
'Tis the wind and nothing more!'

Open here I flung the shutter, when, with many a flirt and flutter,
In there stepped a stately raven of the saintly days of yore.
Not the least obeisance made he; not a minute stopped or stayed he;
But, with mien of lord or lady, perched above my chamber door -
Perched upon a bust of Pallas just above my chamber door -
Perched, and sat, and nothing more.

Then this ebony bird beguiling my sad fancy into smiling,
By the grave and stern decorum of the countenance it wore,
`Though thy crest be shorn and shaven, thou,' I said, `art sure no craven.
Ghastly grim and ancient raven wandering from the nightly shore -
Tell me what thy lordly name is on the Night's Plutonian shore!'
Quoth the raven, `Nevermore.'

To read the rest of the poem, go to
http://www.heise.de/ix/raven/Literature/Lore/TheRaven.html

Student Analysis of the first eight stanzas of "The Raven"

The speaker of this poem is a man who had fallen asleep while reading to escape the grief of the death of someone whom he cared deeply about. The audience is no one in particular. Knowing that Poe's writing was from the 1800s and that most of his writings centered around the mourning of lost loved ones and lovers would allow one to assume that the woman mentioned in this poem was either a lover or a loved one and the death hit close to home. The poem on the literal level is about a man who fell asleep while reading as he tried to escape his grief over the death of a women named Lenore. He was awakened by a tapping at his door and after being dazed for a moment he rose and answered the door only to find darkness greeting him. The next time he opens it, a raven enters and utters a single word: "Nevermore." This indicates the hopelessness of the narrator and leads us to the theme of the poem: "When someone dies, they are gone for good." The tone ("a midnight dreary") suggests sorrow and hopelessness. Words I didn't know: surcease (means "end"); Pallas, which I found out is another name for Athena, the goddess of wisdom; and beguiling, which means to enchant in a deceptive way.

A deeper analysis would also look at the references (or allusions) as well as the rhyme scheme, meter, and word choice. Poe's biographical information might also be used to help understand the poem.

From Reading to Writing

The two poems we've looked at in this chapter are fairly old-fashioned. Not many poets who are writing in the 21st Century write poems in this manner, and you are certainly not expected to write like Wordsworth or Poe. You are expected to write like you, but reading the poets of the past will help you understand the power of word choice (diction), meter, tone, imagery, and so on and choose which techniques you may want to use for your own work.

In future chapters we'll be looking at the work of contemporary poets as well as performance poets. But mostly, you'll be writing your own poems and sharing them with each other. However, if you know the basics of poetry analysis, it will help you when you are discussing your own poems and the poems of your peers.

Rules of Poetry

- Poetry doesn't have to rhyme

- Poetry doesn't have to be pretty
- Poetry doesn't have to be sad or depressing
- Poetry can rhyme
- Poetry can be pretty
- Poetry can be sad and depressing
- Poetry can also be playful
- Poetry can be joyful
- Poetry can be funny
- Poetry can be about important events
- Poetry can be about mundane events
- Poetry can be about anything at all
- Poetry can be written in everyday language.
- Poetry can be written in an elevated, formal style.

There is no wrong or right way to write poetry, but there are some ways to make poetry more effective, and we'll be examining those techniques in the first part of this course. Those same techniques can be used to make your scenes and prose more effective as well.

Blog/Journal Assignment:

Go to Poets.org and find a poem that you like. Write a brief analysis, considering speaker, subject, theme, and tone.

Student Writing Sample

I find that student writers sometimes have difficulty making abstract ideas concrete (more about this later). So I like to bring in my shell collection and have students choose a shell and write about it. Student writer Marissa Moore takes on the persona of a grieving elderly man and brings a somber tone to this poem about a shell:

Smooth with a few ridges folded along your back. I wonder what you look like.
The ocean is my place to see now that my eyes have left me. I feel you and you are strong.
You are cracked near your lips and I see a hazy picture of my childhood crush
who had a scar near her luscious lips. Have you returned to me, my friend?

I twist you over and slide my thumb against your throat,
feeling the dent where a child once laid. Ah, so not my childhood crush
but perhaps my second wife? The struggle you went through alone while my ego took credit
for the child you bore. But the pearls grow up and find better, happier lives.
I wish you had done the same, I wish you would have known better than to stay.

I clutch your shell close to my heart and I wonder what you look like.
Are you as white as the ivory from your wedding gown
or yellow from the cancer that settled deep in your breast?
Or perhaps you're blue from the favorite lake you used to visit.

How strange you should find your way to an ocean.
Perhaps you are just on another quest and I'm holding you back once more.
I lay you back down on the sand though I want to put you in my pocket and carry you home.
I guess old habits die hard.

-- Marissa Moore

Vocabulary

Define the following and add any new words that you have encountered recently:

Context

Lore

Motif

Mundane

Pensive

Persona

Omniscient

Writing Prompts

3. Fill in the blanks.

Today my name is _____

I know _____

_____

There never was a time this was not so.

4.   Complete this sentence:

Writing is …

Chapter Three
Rhythm, Rhyme, and Repetition

We humans are rhythmic beings. Our hearts are little drummers inside us that never stop beating until we're dead. We respond to rhythm. We have cycles. We are attuned to seasons. Even a small child will dance when she hears a beat.

Music, of course, would be meaningless without rhythm. At the beginning of every musical piece, the composer writes two numbers -- one for the number of beats to a measure, and one to show what type of note (half, quarter, etc.) counts as a beat. It's the beat that gives music emotional power as much as the melody. If you ever learned to play the piano, then you probably used a metronome, an instrument that makes a steady beating sound, to help you keep the correct rhythm of the music.

When writing has rhythm, it satisfies something primal in the reader's psyche. We feel at home with the words. Most formal poetry has an internal rhythm similar to musical rhythm. You can hear it and even clap your hands or snap your fingers to the beat.

Meter

In poetry, rhythm is created by patterns of stressed and unstressed syllables. Stressed syllables are pronounced with more intensity than unstressed ones. They are louder and may be said at a higher pitch. Formal poetry often follows a strict rhythmic pattern, but even free verse will usually have some underlying pattern of beats.

Meter is how we measure rhythm in poetry. Stressed and unstressed syllables are arranged in metrical feet of two to three syllables. A line that is five feet long has five units of two or three syllables. Words are chosen carefully to fit into the required number of beats like pieces to a puzzle. The "beats" have different stresses or pulses. Think of the word: elevator. The "el" and "va" are stressed. The other two syllables are not stressed.

Remember the Wordsworth poem you read in an earlier chapter. Here the stressed syllables are in all caps. (The first word "I" is not stressed.)

I WAN/ dered LONE/ ly AS/ a CLOUD.

This type of stress is called an "iamb." The iamb is a type of two-syllable stress: soft - hard. There are four iambs in this line, so we call it iambic tetrameter.

Online research:

Go online and discover the stresses of these metric feet:

trochee --

dactyl --

anapest --

In Shakespeare's day, rhythm was so important that most sonnets and often entire plays were written in a style called "iambic pentameter." Read the first two lines of one of Shakespeare's most famous sonnets and break the lines into iambs:

> *Shall I compare thee to a summer's day?*
> *Thou art more lovely and more temperate:*

So how many feet are in a line of iambic pentameter? _____

Rhymes

Rhymes are a mnemonic device. When you were a child, you heard nursery rhymes, such as this one:

> *Jack and Jill went up the hill*
> *to fetch a pail of water.*
> *Jack fell down and broke his crown.*
> *And Jill came tumbling after.*

From the Mother Goose rhymes and Doctor Seuss stories you heard as a child to the lyrics of songs you've listened to ever since, you've been hearing words used in poetic ways to convey thoughts and feelings for your whole life. And you can remember them because rhymes help you know what to expect.

Rhyme, of course, occurs when two words sound the same: "name" and "tame." But rhyme can be more complex than the standard "I love to look at the moon/and sing a soulful tune." Rhymes can be "near rhymes," which means that the words are not a perfect rhyme but fairly close, such as "laughter" and "daughter." Rhymes don't necessarily need to be at the end of the line either. They can be interior rhymes, which are more subtle, but sometimes more interesting. Notice the "near rhyme" of the second and fourth lines in "Jack and Jill" ("water" and "after") as well as the interior rhyme in the first and third lines.

When we talk about rhyme scheme, we describe it by assigning each ending word of a line an alphabetical letter. For instance in Wordsworth's poem "I wandered lonely as a cloud," the rhyme scheme is a-b-a-b-c-c. The first line rhymes with the third line. The second line rhymes with the fourth line. And the last two lines are what we call a couplet: they rhyme with each other.

Here's a simple rhyme scheme in a poem divided into quatrains (four line stanzas):

Richard Cory

by Edward Arlington Robinson

Whenever Richard Cory went down town,	A
We people on the pavement looked at him:	B
He was a gentleman from sole to crown,	A
Clean favored, and imperially slim.	B
And he was always quietly arrayed,	C
And he was always human when he talked;	D
But still he fluttered pulses when he said,	C (near rhyme)
'Good-morning,' and he glittered when he walked.	D
And he was rich - yes, richer than a king -	E
And admirably schooled in every grace:	F
In fine, we thought that he was everything	E
To make us wish that we were in his place.	F
So on we worked, and waited for the light,	G
And went without the meat, and cursed the bread;	H
And Richard Cory, one calm summer night,	G
Went home and put a bullet through his head.	H

For a musical variation of this poem, look up the song "Richard Cory" by singer/songwriters Paul Simon and Art Garfunkel.

Some contemporary poets still write in a formal style, but there is less emphasis on rhythm and rhyme today. Modern poems often don't rhyme or conform to a set meter, and line length can be quite varied. However, you can still find strong examples of rhyme and rhythm in song and rap lyrics, and performance poets generally place a greater emphasis on rhyme and rhythm in their work.

Sound

Rhythm and rhyme are responsible for the sound of poetry. And sound is what makes a poem a poem. Sound comes from the way the words are put together, the way they rub against each other, the way they evoke feelings in the reader, independent of their meaning. This is why every single word in a poem is important.

Read the following poem, "Jabberwocky" by Lewis Carroll and notice how the sounds of the words create a feeling, an image in your mind, even though you have no idea what many of the words mean!

Jabberwocky

By Lewis Carroll

Twas brillig, and the slithy toves
* Did gyre and gimble in the wabe:*
All mimsy were the borogoves,
* And the mome raths outgrabe.*

"Beware the Jabberwock, my son!
* The jaws that bite, the claws that catch!*
Beware the Jubjub bird, and shun
* The frumious Bandersnatch!"*

He took his vorpal sword in hand:
* Long time the manxome foe he sought --*
So rested he by the Tumtum tree,
* And stood awhile in thought.*

And, as in uffish thought he stood,
* The Jabberwock, with eyes of flame,*
Came whiffling through the tulgey wood,
* And burbled as it came!*

One, two! One, two! And through and through

The vorpal blade went snicker-snack!
He left it dead, and with its head
He went galumphing back.

"And, has thou slain the Jabberwock?
Come to my arms, my beamish boy!
O frabjous day! Callooh! Callay!'
He chortled in his joy.

`Twas brillig, and the slithy toves
Did gyre and gimble in the wabe;
All mimsy were the borogoves,
And the mome raths outgrabe.

Alliteration, Consonance, Assonance

In addition to rhythm and rhyme, poets (and all writers) have other techniques they can use to create a particular effect with sound.

- Alliteration is the repetition of initial sounds in words that are next to each other or in close proximity. Example: "Bertha is big, bad and beautiful."
- Consonance is the repetition of consonants in a line, such as these lines by Alfred Lord Tennyson: "The moan of doves in immemorial elms,/ and murmuring of innumerable bees."
- Assonance occurs when a vowel sound is repeated as in "sweet sleep"—which is also alliterative!

Assignments:

1. Write three lines: one using alliteration, one using consonance, and one using assonance.

_____

_____

_____

2. If you don't know what the word "onomatopoeia" means, look it up. Provide at least three example:

Repetition

Another technique for creating a feeling of rhythm is to repeat lines. What do you think makes Martin Luther King Junior's "I Have a Dream" speech so powerful? It's not just the ideas, it's the way he says them. That speech has a refrain that sticks in the mind. Poets know the power of repetition. They may repeat a word, a line, or two lines, as in a song refrain.

Research Assignment:

Look up a poem by one of these traditional poets: Christina Rossetti, Percy Shelley, William Wordsworth, John Keats, Lord Byron, Samuel Taylor Coleridge, Phillis Wheatley, or Elizabeth Barrett Browning. Copy the poem and figure out the rhyme scheme. Share the poem with your classmates or writing group.

Blog/Journal Assignment:

At some point during this unit on sound, try to go to a poetry reading or a slam poetry performance. You can also find some great examples online if it's not possible to see one live. Write a response incorporating the ideas about poetry that we are studying in this unit, and include examples.

Student Writing

Following is poem that follows a repetition fill-in-the-blank formula:

I Am

I am a traveler in the sifting sands of the desert
I wonder where the brilliant blue green-oasis lies awaiting me
I hear nothing but the wind coursing through the sand
I see a mirage of my home
I want something new to experience
I am a wanderer in my own life

I pretend that nothing bothers me
I feel the blistering heat of the sun on my neck
I touch the fabric of my chakra
I worry too much
I cry not as often as I should
I am one sunburned human being

I understand very little
I say either too little or too much
I try to persevere
I hope to be humble
I am two people

-- Alexander Murphy

Poetry is a vehicle for individual expression. Even when writing a fill-in-the-blank poem, each poet expresses herself or himself uniquely:

Who I Am

I am myself
I wonder why I feel like I don't belong
I hear all these opinions
I see what everyone else is like
I want to be like them
I am myself

I pretend to be anyone else
I feel so confused when I pretend
I touch on the thoughts of who I am
I worry how I'll ever fit in
I cry when they laugh
I am myself

I understand that being me is great
I say "I don't care what they say"
I try to make it true
I hope I can stay true to me
I am, and always will be, myself

-- Gabrielle Porter

Here's a poem that uses repetition of the first line of each stanza to create rhythm.

Little Lion Boy

Little lion boy
Raised to be wild
With dangerous instinct
How fierce you are
When your mane flows
As you toss your head back
In naive offense
But how sweet you are
When you're curled beside me
Fast asleep with feral dreams
And your fur matted down
Making you seem so much smaller.

Little lion boy
Stalking elusive prey
With your head held high
Though you question your ability
Because sometimes you go hungry

How brave you are
To keep going each day
But how scared you are
When you look at me
With wide and curious eyes
Appearing so much more innocent.

Little lion boy
Born of a different world
Where survival of the fittest is the law
And sometimes surviving
Is the hardest task you do all day
How strong you are
To protect the frail
But how weak you are
Not to take the good you've been given
Believing you are so much worse off.

-- Rebecca Fisher

This student writer uses a slightly different approach by repeating just the first word of each stanza. He also incorporates rhyme.

Reflections

Reflections of a life not yet lived;
Formation of self
Means ability to forgive.

Reflections of a planet halved;
The Sun and Moon and stars cannot shine bright enough
To shed light in every dark place, where going got tough.

Reflections of life, the illusion;
Here one minute, gone the next instant,
Offering a gift of misguided delusion.

Reflections of shadows, spaces unknown;
Impeding lightness, blocking progress,
Casting doubt where certainty'd grown.

Reflection unreflected;
You've created resolution:
Thought, fairness, hope must be protected.

-- Grady Garrison

Finally, here is a poem from a fun exercise we do in my classes. In this exercise, you choose a word or a phrase and you begin every line of the poem with the word or phrase until the last couple of lines.

Love

If you love me, tell me
If you love me, I will be there
If you love me, show me
If you love me, I wouldn't know
If you love me, express it to the world
If you love me, then why is my finger bare?
If you love me, come to me
If you love me, roses ... I love roses
If you love me, chivalry is still alive
If you love me, be addicted
If you love me, celebrate
If you love me, be there
If you love me, appreciate
If you love me, love with love stronger than deep, but ...
If you knew me, you would know,
falling in love with me would not be the best way to go.

-- Jessica Dianna Neal

Vocabulary

Define the following and add any new words that you have encountered recently:

Arrayed

Meter

Mnemonic device

Onomatopoeia

Quatrain

Writing Prompts

1. Fill in the blanks to create a repetition poem:

    I am

    I wonder

    I hear

    I see

    I want

    I am

    I pretend

    I feel

    I touch

    I worry

    I cry

    I am

I understand

I say

I try

I hope

I am

2.   Choose a word or phrase and write eight or more lines beginning with that word or phrase. You can change it up (or not) when you get to the last two lines.

3.   The Observation Poem

Take your journal and go outside. Find a place to sit away from other people – under a tree, beside a pond, on a bench. Close your eyes and notice. What do you hear? What do you smell? How does the air feel? Is there a breeze? Don't ignore "human-made" impressions.

Now open your eyes and write down the answers to the questions.

Now look around you. What do you see? Find something to observe closely. Describe it. Avoid judgment words such as ugly, beautiful, nice, pleasant. Imagine you are a camera.

Now that you've written down all your impressions, start making a poem out of it. Remember, rhyming is not important. What feelings or thoughts did this experience inspire in you?

Chapter Four
Figurative Language

A figure of speech is a way of saying something that helps your listener understand what you mean but is not to be taken literally. In an office setting, we might say a person "wears different hats," meaning that person takes on different roles. When people say, "the sky's the limit," they are probably not really saying anything about the sky. They mean that anything is possible.

Every day we use figures of speech. They're so common they usually pass by us unnoticed. Language and especially figures of speech are always changing to reflect the times. What are some figures of speech or expressions common to you and your friends?

_____

_____

_____

Figures of speech can become dated, they can become clichés, and they can be confusing. But for writers, figures of speech are an important element of the creative process. In fact, there is a formal system of figures of speech that poets, especially, rely on when trying to express themselves.

Simile and Metaphor

A simile and a metaphor do essentially the same thing: they compare two unlike things, which helps the reader *get* it. Similes and metaphors make language fun. They exercise your brain.

As you probably know, the difference is that similes use the words "like" or "as" to compare two things, as in "My love is like a red, red rose." If the poet, Robert Burns, had instead written, "My love is a red, red rose," then he would be using a metaphor.

Read the following quotation from writer E.L. Doctorow: "Writing is an exploration. You start from nothing and learn as you go. … Writing is like driving at night in the fog. You can only see as far as your headlights, but you can make the whole trip that way. ... Writing is a socially acceptable form of schizophrenia." Doctorow uses simile and metaphor to more clearly express what he wants to say about the act and process of writing.

- The first statement is a metaphor: "Writing is an exploration."
- Then he uses a simile: "Writing is like driving at night in the fog."
- Then he goes back to a metaphor: "Writing is a socially acceptable form of schizophrenia."

Shakespeare used many metaphors. One of his most famous is "All the world's a stage" from the play *As You Like It*. In this speech he develops his metaphor into a lengthy analogy, comparing life to a play. Read the speech below:

"All the world's a stage,
And all the men and women merely players;
They have their exits and their entrances;
And one man in his time plays many parts,
His acts being seven ages. At first the infant,
Mewling and puking in the nurse's arms;
And then the whining school-boy, with his satchel
And shining morning face, creeping like snail
Unwillingly to school. And then the lover,
Sighing like furnace, with a woeful ballad
Made to his mistress' eyebrow. Then a soldier,
Full of strange oaths, and bearded like the pard,
Jealous in honour, sudden and quick in quarrel,
Seeking the bubble reputation
Even in the cannon's mouth. And then the justice,
In fair round belly with good capon lin'd,
With eyes severe and beard of formal cut,
Full of wise saws and modern instances;
And so he plays his part. The sixth age shifts
Into the lean and slipper'd pantaloon,
With spectacles on nose and pouch on side;
His youthful hose, well sav'd, a world too wide
For his shrunk shank; and his big manly voice,
Turning again toward childish treble, pipes
And whistles in his sound. Last scene of all,
That ends this strange eventful history,

Is second childishness and mere oblivion;
Sans teeth, sans eyes, sans taste, sans everything."

In addition to the overall analogy, you can find several metaphors and similes in the speech.

Write down some metaphors and similes of your own. If you need some help, try these prompts:

My love is like...

I danced like...

He screamed like...

This day is...

My heart is...

Our friendship is...

Hyperbole and Understatement

How many times have you said something like, "That was the worst movie ever made" or "That was the most delicious food I ever ate in my life" or "That was the hardest test on the planet"? You probably use these kinds of phrases pretty frequently. This type of speech is called hyperbole. We use hyperbole a lot in our everyday speech. Writers use hyperbole, too. It often adds humor to a piece of writing.

Mark Twain was famous for hyperbole as demonstrated in his tall tale, "The Celebrated Jumping Frog of Calaveras County" about a gambler and his trained frog:

"He ketched a frog one day, and took him home, and said he cal'klated to edercate him; and so he never done nothing for three months but set in his back yard and learn that frog to jump. And you bet you he did learn him too. He'd give him a little punch behind, and the next minute you'd see that frog whirling in the air like a doughnut—see him turn one summerset, or may be a couple, if he got a good start, and come down flatfooted and all right, like a cat."

The comic writer Dave Barry uses hyperbole to great effect in his columns for the *Miami Herald*. In a column about playing baseball with former professional players for a charity event, Barry writes, "The pitcher I faced was Al 'The Mad Hungarian' Hrabosky, who still looks as though he has just been kicked out of the Institute for the Criminally Insane for being a little TOO insane, and who can still throw pretty hard (by which I mean "faster than light"). He struck me out on three pitches. I was still swinging at the last one when Hrabosky was in the showers" (July 15, 2013).

Understatement is just the opposite of hyperbole. It is when we deliberately underplay something. If a person who has just saved your life modestly says, "Oh, it was nothing," you would likely find that to be an understatement. Writers may use understatement in a humorous manner as well or they may use it to tell us something about a character.

Personification

Personification means giving human qualities such as feelings, thoughts or action to non-living objects like houses or to abstract ideas such as love. A similar term is anthropomorphism, which generally applies to deities (gods and goddesses) and animals.

Emily Dickinson often used personification in her poetry. Here's one of my favorite examples:

"Hope" is the thing with feathers -
That perches in the soul -
And sings the tune without the words -
And never stops - at all -

And sweetest - in the Gale - is heard -
And sore must be the storm -
That could abash the little Bird
That kept so many warm -

I've heard it in the chillest land -
And on the strangest Sea -
Yet - never - in Extremity,
It asked a crumb - of me.

Blog/Journal Assignment:

Look around you at the inanimate objects or phenomena that you encounter every day, and in your blog, write five to ten examples of personification.

Examples:

The wind howled like a broken-hearted lover.

The seatbelt buzzer pestered me until I finally obeyed it.

The worried clock watched over me.

The sweet berries begged to be eaten.

The sunlight kissed my face.

Student Writing Samples

The following poem is an analogy about an unhappy relationship. The poet also uses repetition and word play to great effect.

Did they tell the lamb?
Did they tell her how the lion would lie down with her?
I bet they didn't
I bet the lamb didn't get much sleep

No one warned the poor lamb
No one explained just what the lion, the lyin', was gonna do
They told the lion I'm sure
They told the lion how it would all go down

He was the only one who needed to know
He was the only one, the only one
I can only imagine the lamb's fright
I can only imagine the single bleat in an echoing roar

Did they tell the lamb?
Did they tell her how the lion would lie down with her?
I bet they didn't
I bet the lamb didn't get much sleep

No one warned the poor lamb
No one explained just what the lion, the lyin', was gonna do
No one except the lion
No one except the lion warned the poor lamb
Told the lamb what he was gonna do
Told the lamb that it was gonna be okay
I bet it wasn't
I bet the lamb didn't get much sleep

-- Rebecca Fisher

Here is an example of personification by the same poet:

Look! Look! Do you see?
The trees are bleeding red.
Leaves drip off and dry to crust
But they don't seem to notice their own death.
"In green veins flows crimson.
That is the way," you chide,
"That is how it will always be."
A withering demise
Collapsing against the hard earth
When they are too fragile to stand back up.
Firm branches grip stubbornly to flaccid life
As the wind coaxes them to the ground.
Skeletons rattle against the stone
Littering the streets with corpses
But no one seems to notice this seasonal genocide:
Too busy looking up
Because we are scared to look down.

-- Rebecca Fisher

Two more examples of personification:

Karma

Karma going around and around,
laughing at everyone she sees,
handing out rewards and punishments,
never heard or seen, dark and mysterious.

"What goes around comes around," they say.
"See you soon," she says to me.

Karma, going around and around,
feared by some, worshipped by others.
She'll come to you, one reason or another.
Never lost, but never in the right direction.

"What goes around comes around."
In a circle she likes to go.

-- Gabrielle Porter

Lady Luck

Lady Luck is fleeting and fickle.
When she graces you with her presence,
she may slap you in the face,
or she may gift you with presents.
Her long, blond, silken, velvet hair
is sure to draw attention
and when your friends see you dating her
they will surely have to mention
that your face has a heavenly glow
and your demeanor is uplifting
effect of gazing in her eyes
of gold and silver glinting.

-- Jeffrey Harris

Vocabulary

Define the following and add any new words that you have encountered recently:

Abash

Analogy

Anthropomorphism

Hyperbole

Personification

Writing Prompts

1. Fill in the blanks of this metaphor/simile group poem. Read your responses one after the other to create a group poem effect. (You can go one stanza at a time or read the whole poem.)

If laughter had a taste, it would taste like _____

and it would _____

and _____

all day long.

If life were a dance, it would be the _____

and I would _____

and _____

all day long.

If sorrow were a sound, it would sound like _____

and it would _____

and_____

all day long

If love were a smell, it would smell like _____

and it would _____

and _____

all day long.

2. Life Metaphor Poem: Write down five things you have done in your life and then add a simile to each one.

Example: "I drove my first car like an astronaut flying a rocket."

3. Choose an emotion and do a free write, writing down all the images, colors, and feelings that the emotion creates inside you. Now take those images and write a 5- to 8-line poem about the emotion. Don't use the word for the emotion or a synonym for the word.

4. Personification Poem: Choose a quality (joy, success, rage, etc.) or an inanimate object (house, car, desk) and give it a personality. Let it be someone.

Chapter Five
The Purposes of Poetry

When you write an essay for school, you know what the purpose is: to demonstrate your knowledge of a topic, to demonstrate your ability to interpret or analyze information about the topic, and/or to form a coherent and convincing argument dealing with that topic. When you write a letter or an email, you are generally passing along information. When you text message or respond to someone's blog or Facebook post, you are engaging in communication with someone.

But what purpose does poetry serve? The answer is that poetry serves different purposes, depending on your needs at the time. Poetry can be a clever way to tell a story, one that will get your listeners' attention and help them remember it. Poetry is the time-honored method for expressing our emotions in a way that other people will understand and respond to. Poetry is also useful for protesting social or personal injustice.

Poets over the ages have used poetry for a number of purposes. They have used poetry to express love, to protest injustice, to rail against the gods, to tell the stories of heroes and heroines, to create word pictures, mark important events, and any number of other things.

In this poem, poet Meri Culp memorializes those who died in a plane crash:

What They Left Behind: The Malaysian Airlines Crash, 7-17-14

A lavender baby blanket curl-covers ash,
a small fire still licking the edges of a popped-open carry-on,

shocking pink, holding its form, spilling a scatter of playing cards,
clipped cash, all bets are off, folding into a silver watch,

broken, its face stuck on a time of wrist attachment,
blue skies, crayoned coloring books, stay in the lines,

jet streaming clouds, soft, animal-shaped,
a leg-twisted stuffed animal, grounded,

keeps smiling its silly monkey grin,
passports hissing smoke, a hairbrush bristling.

Painting Pictures with Poetry

The most effective poems are often based on images, and these poems, in turn, create images in the readers' or listeners' minds. Abstract ideas—love, valor, sorrow, grief, and so on—are understood by everyone to different extents and in different ways, but in order to say something intelligible about these ideas you must use specific sensory details. It's a paradox that universal ideas or feelings must be communicated through specific, concrete and individualized details, but that seems to be the way we are wired.

The most common sensory details are visual images. Look around. What do you see? Do any of these images have a symbolic meaning? Does something you see remind you of something else?

An imagistic poem can:

- Tell a story
- Create a mood
- Convey a feeling
- Provide a moral
- Or simply paint a picture

One way to incorporate concrete images is to focus on an object. An object can turn into a symbol for an abstract idea such as love, loneliness or aging. Or writing about an object may provide you with an opportunity to explore your feelings about the object.

Concrete vs. Abstract

Sometimes beginning poets get hung up trying to write about deep emotions or complicated ideas. This kind of writing can become abstract, and while it may be meaningful to the poet, the full import of the meaning is not always transmitted to the reader. For instance, what does "you are so beautiful" really mean? Everyone has a different idea of what is beautiful. That statement doesn't really communicate much to the reader. "My love is like a red, red rose," on the other hand, is a poetic line that transmits an idea we can see and smell.

Even when writing about abstract ideas such as "heaven" or "death," a good poet will make those ideas concrete by using images. Percy Bysshe Shelley describes both death and sleep using images in this excerpt from his poem "Queen Mab."

How wonderful is Death,
Death, and his brother Sleep!
One, pale as yonder waning moon
With lips of lurid blue;
The other, rosy as the morn
When throned on ocean's wave
It blushes o'er the world;
Yet both so passing wonderful!

You can connect to your reader through concrete images in a way that is often missing with more abstract terms such as "love," "peace," or "hurt." Concrete images and sensory details make poetry more vivid. They help it to come alive for the readers. Writers use the senses of taste, touch, hearing, sight, and smell to enable readers to experience what they experience or to help themselves get in touch with deep memories and the feelings associated with those memories.

Poetry as a Tool for Self Discovery

Poetic images sometimes come from our subconscious minds. We find meaning in the images of our dreams and the symbols of our lives. Self-discovery is a process that never really ends, for we change and evolve as we age. Because poetry uses symbols and relies on images, it can be a key to learning about the being (or beings) inside you—in both an existential and a microbial sense!

Poetry as Protest

In any society, the dominant culture may often drown out the voices of marginalized or oppressed groups. Poetry has been used for much of the 20th century to give marginalized people a voice. Poetry is the perfect outlet for the hurt and outrage that comes from injustice or poor social conditions.

You've probably come across this poem by Langston Hughes at some point, but have you stopped to think what the poem is really about? Consider that the poem was written in 1951, shortly before the Civil Rights Movement, when Black Americans were denied educational opportunities, housing, and jobs in most places in America. This poem serves as an outcry against that injustice and perhaps a warning as well.

What happens to a dream deferred?
Does it dry up
like a raisin in the sun?
Or fester like a sore--
And then run?
Does it stink like rotten meat?
Or crust and sugar over--
like a syrupy sweet?
Maybe it just sags
like a heavy load.
Or does it explode?

Poetry can also be used to express anger or pain over personal injustice, as when someone betrays you or hurts your feelings. In most cases, a poem provides a safe outlet for your emotions. However, some poets have gone to jail or been killed for writing the truth in their poetry.

Pretend

One of the joys of being a writer is that you don't always have to be yourself. You can step into someone else's shoes and imagine what it's like to be that person. Sometimes being a writer is like being an actor. You put on a costume of words and—if you want to—you can die tragically and then get up and walk away after the curtain has closed.

Poets sometimes write as themselves, but other times they take on the voice and attitudes of another person. In the song "All I Wanna Do," Sheryl Crow takes on the persona of someone at a bar commenting on the other patrons.

Persona poems allow you to be younger or older. You can be a person of a different ethnicity or gender. Or you can take on the voice of a dead person as Edgar Lee Masters does in *Spoon River Anthology*.

Expressing Deep Emotions

Poetry is all about feelings. There must be more than a billion love poems out there. Poetry is also about other emotions: hate, fear, joy, spiritual ecstasy, friendship, satisfaction, wonder and so on.

But all of the above are abstract terms and you've already learned that abstract terms are not always as effective as concrete images. It takes some thought to be able to write a poem about a deep emotion and not get too abstract. And yet it can be done.

One form of poetry that was used by the Ancient Greeks to express reverence or respect was the "ode." This was generally a long poem of praise about a person. But you can also write an ode to an animal or an object as John Keats does in "Ode to a Nightingale."

This entire poem is eight stanzas long. Here are the final three stanzas. Note that each stanza is 10 lines with an ABABCDECDE rhyme scheme. The poem begins with the speaker wanting to die, but listening to the bird's joyful song ("such an ecstasy) disrupts his train of thought.

Darkling I listen; and, for many a time
I have been half in love with easeful Death,
Call'd him soft names in many a musèd rhyme,
To take into the air my quiet breath;
Now more than ever seems it rich to die,
To cease upon the midnight with no pain,
While thou art pouring forth thy soul abroad
In such an ecstasy!
Still wouldst thou sing, and I have ears in vain—
To thy high requiem become a sod.

Thou wast not born for death, immortal Bird!
No hungry generations tread thee down;
The voice I hear this passing night was heard
In ancient days by emperor and clown:
Perhaps the self-same song that found a path
Through the sad heart of Ruth, when, sick for home,
She stood in tears amid the alien corn;
The same that ofttimes hath
Charm'd magic casements, opening on the foam
Of perilous seas, in faery lands forlorn.

Forlorn! the very word is like a bell
To toll me back from thee to my sole self!
Adieu! the fancy cannot cheat so well
As she is famed to do, deceiving elf.
Adieu! adieu! thy plaintive anthem fades
  Past the near meadows, over the still stream,
  Up the hill-side; and now 'tis buried deep
  In the next valley-glades:
  Was it a vision, or a waking dream?
    Fled is that music:—do I wake or sleep?

Blog/Journal Assignment:

Use your search engine and put in the words "child" and "poverty." Do a little research on this issue or another issue that is important to you. Then write a poem about it.

Student Writing Samples

Concrete objects help us to convey abstract ideas. Here is a poem about an object that shows the effects of time.

Paperweight

What once was light blue and clear
now has faded and aged
until it has taken on a milky white facade.
Cracks which started on the surface of the glass
have slowly worked their way to the core,
like thin fingers stretching outward.
What was once young and smooth is no longer
the same as that which sits on my dusty desk,
day after day, year after year,
Weighed down by responsibility and clouded by time.

--Alexander Murphy

The following is an example of a student poet having fun with the ode format:

Oyster of Tides

A requiem for thee, young oyster,
for at one time you laid in praise of the sunlight
the currents of tides and sediment tore at
the knuckles of your shell; but you remained safe,
you remained sealed in fortitude and chaste to the torment
of the ocean. But your exterior
has been penetrated by a lowly slug.

woe to your sunstealer, young oyster.

-- Ridge Graham

Here's an example of a persona poem from a student, who assumed the role of "advice-columnist." Notice the compilation of sensory details that bring the reader into the experience.

Advice to a Child

Be blessed with the fever,
That arrives in spring,
And lasts through summer.

Slide through fences,
And dream about witches,
Snag shirts on bent chicken wire.

Sleep in bunk beds,
Wear shirts to your shins,
Walk barefoot on cold wood.

Scramble around the house
Where the witches brew,
Hope eyes closed they don't catch you.

Swim in the dark
With the pool light glowing
Please, embrace never knowing,

And crash on shag carpets
Under fluffy white towels…

And try not to notice
your grown-ups' worry lines.

-- Celina Chapin

The following poem was inspired by an aroma:

Cinnamon
the essence of cinnamon is familiarity
mothers at the oven hold their hands out

to their children clamoring "let me smell, let me smell"
and they add inches to their height, their limbs lengthen, their faces slender

the mother holds fast
she imagines a mess of youthful innocence; she rubs her cloth over
the counter, cleaning honey handprints left
twenty years ago

and somewhere fifty states away a man
stands in his kitchen and lifts the box
and his eyes close -- the scent he recognizes

-- Anna Fulghum

Here's a repetition poem, expressing a strong emotion:

Call me when you're sober.
Call me when this B.S is over.
Call me when you're done with games.
Call me when you're ready to take some blame.
Call me when you feel the hole.
Call me when you realize what you stole.
Call me when you run out of friends.
Call me when you've realized this wasn't the end.
Call me when you've exhausted every escape.
Call me when every single muscle aches.
Call me when the memories make you brutally weep.
Call me when you ache for love that runs eternally deep.
Call me when even the moon can't lift the black.
Call me when you're ready to come back.

-- D'Avva Holiday

This poem was inspired by a walk through the cemetery. Notice the dark, somber tone.

Graveyard Walk

Smoke and ash --
that's all that remains

it swarmed the town like a plague
bent on its path of destruction
but there was nothing left
no souls to consume
no lives to extinguish
just empty vessels
shadows
doomed to wander alone
their sparks buried
alongside their men
the men that died so they could live
but what was left for them
to carry out alone
smoke and ash
burned them down
but they were already dead.

-- Shannon Verity

The following poem conveys an entirely different sense with images of happiness and childhood joy. It shows us what joy is through sensory details.

Spinning Basket

Basket on wheels
My body wrapped in warm sheets
And colored towels
Aroma of tide and dryer sheets,
Women in Walmart perfume
Wiping sweat from their brows
And continuing with their labors.

Open cup of tapioca pudding,
Bubbles running through my teeth
And around my tongue
Momma reaches over me
Remarks that I should be careful
And grabs her bag of darks
She smells of patchouli and fresh cut grass.

"Now?" I ask, mouth bubbling
With the last spoonful of pudding,
"Not yet, baby," she whispers

Eyes shifting to the lady loading
Folded clothes into baskets
Placing them in her Lincoln
Grabbing her bag of quarters and
July issue of Cosmo.

She goes, leaving her aura of hard work
And tired thought
That quickly evaporates with the break
Of Momma's sneaky smile as
She grabs the basket and begins
To run.

My hair blows back off my neck,
Body quickly lightened
With the speed of spinning wheels,
She twirls me, the room surrounding
a giant swirl of distant reality,
I'm drunk on Tide and her mellow
Laugh, her patchouli and perspiration,
Willingly trapped in this spinning
Basket,
On a carousel of memories.

--Kelsey Armour

We'll end this Student Writing Sample with a "self-portrait" poem. This comes from an exercise we do in my classes, using mirrors.

Tread lightly, this one is dangerous.
The faint lift in her brow, the slight tilt to her smile.
Be wary, this one is wild.

The nonchalance in her stance, the annoyance in her glance,
she doesn't care about you or your existence
Hold fast, breathe shallow, and be careful of the depths of those dark brown orbs.
Those two gems could both ignite and chill, excite the heart and leave it forever still.
Watch your every move, this one might be crazy.

Yet we stare,
Stare endlessly into the dark eyes that tell no lies and the hurt,
the hurt that is lying just behind the shimmer of the iris, the lies,
that linger about the heart that is guarded by a layer of ice so deep, the tears
that she told herself she would not shed as she fell asleep, the hope

that tries to escape so often yet falls to her feet, the fear
that she will never find what she craves the most.
Be wary, this one is wild.

She is cultured, poised, creative chaos,
tailored, mangled, marred, beauty,
expressive, consoling, peaceful depression,
manic, raging, violent joy
rebellious, unforgiving, thoughtful love.
Tread carefully, this one is dangerous.

-- D'Avva Holiday

Vocabulary

Define the following and add any new words that you have encountered recently:

Marginalize

Paradox

Persona

Sensory

Writing Prompts

1. Make a list of images from your childhood (i.e., swing sets, clover fields, basketball courts, pine trees, etc.) Now think back to how you felt as a child. When were you happiest? Close your eyes and try to "see" what you were doing at the time. Write a poem that tells a story from your childhood using these images.

2.   Choose an object that is meaningful to you and write an ode to it.

3.   Take a walk through a cemetery and write a persona poem from the point of view of one of the dead. Or meditate on the transitory nature of life and write a poem about it.

4.   Many painters are famous for their self-portraits. But poets can write self-portraits as well. Here is a method to try. Take a hand mirror and look at your face. (If you don't have a hand mirror, you can look into a wall mirror.) What do you see there? What do your eyes tell you? Try to be objective and not critical. Write down the details. What does your face tell us about the person inside? Who is that person? Where has she been? Where is he going? Now write a poem based on the images in the mirror.

Chapter Six
Forms of Poetry

The poet Dana Goia said, "Tradition is not . . . a library or museum the artist plunders. It is the endless conversation between the living and the dead. Young artists enter into this conversation passionately--not merely intellectually, though study and analysis play a part. They live and breathe it. Tradition is not a public building. It is a love affair."

Formal poetry doesn't require rhyme, but in general you will find that the rhyme scheme in formal poetry is built into the structure. As you learned in an earlier lesson, we can create a "scheme" for a rhyming poem.

Read the poem below:

First Fig

by Edna St. Vincent Millay

My candle burns at both ends;
It will not last the night;
But ah, my foes, and oh, my friends --
It gives a lovely light!

What is the rhyme scheme of this quatrain? _____

Ballads

Ballads are close relatives to song. These narrative poems often tell a story about legendary figures such as Robin Hood or the lovers "Frankie and Johnny." Many ballads can be sung and are generally written in ballad meter. The rhyme scheme is often ABCB.

Bold Robin Hood said to his jolly bowmen,
Pray tarry you here in this grove;
* And see that you all observe well my call,*
While thorough the forest I rove.

The stanzas are usually couplets or quatrains, but not always.

Sonnets

When we think of sonnets, we may think of Shakespeare and Elizabeth Barrett Browning, but many poets today still enjoy the sonnet form though they may not always adhere to its strict rhyme scheme. The following sonnet has a timeless quality in its portrayal of deep, passionate love.

How do I love thee?

By Elizabeth Barrett Browning

How do I love thee? Let me count the ways.
I love thee to the depth and breadth and height
My soul can reach, when feeling out of sight
For the ends of being and ideal grace.
I love thee to the level of every day's
Most quiet need, by sun and candle-light.
I love thee freely, as men strive for right.
I love thee purely, as they turn from praise.
I love thee with the passion put to use
In my old griefs, and with my childhood's faith.
I love thee with a love I seemed to lose
With my lost saints. I love thee with the breath,
Smiles, tears, of all my life; and, if God choose,
I shall but love thee better after death.

English sonnets are fourteen lines long and usually have a set rhyme pattern of ABABABAB CDE CDE or ABAB CDCD EFEF GG.

Another form developed in Italy with a slightly different rhyming pattern: ABBA ABBA CDECDE (or CDCCDC).

In Shakespeare's sonnets, each line is written in iambic pentameter and contains ten syllables.

My mistress' eyes are nothing like the sun

by William Shakespeare

My mistress' eyes are nothing like the sun;
Coral is far more red than her lips' red;
If snow be white, why then her breasts are dun;
If hairs be wires, black wires grow on her head.

I have seen roses damask'd, red and white,
But no such roses see I in her cheeks;
And in some perfumes is there more delight
Than in the breath that from my mistress reeks.
I love to hear her speak, yet well I know
That music hath a far more pleasing sound;
I grant I never saw a goddess go;
My mistress, when she walks, treads on the ground:
And yet, by heaven, I think my love as rare
As any she belied with false compare.

Spend some time thinking of a suitable topic for a sonnet. Have you ever been in love? Perhaps you could describe the one you love in a sonnet form? Or have you had an experience where something happened that surprised you? Have you had a problem or do you have one now that might lend itself to this form? Sonnets sometimes present a problem in the first eight lines and then solve it in the next six lines.

Remember you can play with the rhyme scheme, but try to get it into a structure that someone else can recognize as a sonnet.

Haiku

Haiku is a Japanese form that many poets enjoy. The form does not depend on rhyme or meter, but rather on syllables. The standard haiku format is:

One line of five syllables

One line of seven syllables

One line of five syllables

For example:

Light falls on green trees
Ferns bend over, touch the ground
Summer is now here

Remember that this syllable count is a guideline, and can be bent without breaking, like a shoot of bamboo. Even Basho, the original Haiku master, did not always adhere precisely to this convention.

Informal Poetry

The first major poet to break away from formal, structured poetry was Walt Whitman, who was born in 1819. Whitman believed that America should have a poetry of its own and not imitate the

British poets. He was a great proponent of equality and democratic values. He felt that poetry should be expressive and free of constraints.

We call this type of writing free verse because it does not conform to a rigid structure. Free verse does not have regular rhymes found at the end of each line. There may be rhyme in free verse, but it will be used with greater freedom. In addition, there is not a fixed meter; free verse is characterized instead by a regular rhythmic cadence.

Read this excerpt from Whitman's "I Sing the Body Electric."

A man's body at auction,
(For before the war I often go to the slave-mart and watch the sale,)
I help the auctioneer, the sloven does not half know his business.

Gentlemen look on this wonder,
Whatever the bids of the bidders they cannot be high enough for it,
For it the globe lay preparing quintillions of years without one animal or plant,
For it the revolving cycles truly and steadily roll'd.

In this head the all-baffling brain,
In it and below it the makings of heroes.

Examine these limbs, red, black, or white, they are cunning in tendon and nerve,
They shall be stript that you may see them.
Exquisite senses, life-lit eyes, pluck, volition,
Flakes of breast-muscle, pliant backbone and neck, flesh not flabby, good-sized arms and legs,
And wonders within there yet.

Within there runs blood,
The same old blood! the same red-running blood!
There swells and jets a heart, there all passions, desires, reachings, aspirations,
(Do you think they are not there because they are not express'd in
parlors and lecture-rooms?)

This is not only one man, this the father of those who shall be fathers in their turns,
In him the start of populous states and rich republics,
Of him countless immortal lives with countless embodiments and enjoyments.

How do you know who shall come from the offspring of his offspring through the centuries?

(Who might you find you have come from yourself, if you could trace
back through the centuries?)

In this excerpt from the poem, Whitman uses irony to convey his abolitionist sentiments. Notice how he seems to take on the role of the auctioneer, the person who is actually selling the slaves. However, by taking on this role, he actually demonstrates the incalculable worth of each human being. In the last stanza, Whitman is prescient (pre-seeing). It's as if he can look into the future to a time when the descendants of these slaves will be writers, actors, business executives, and even the President of the United States. At the time this idea would have been unimaginable to many people.

Revolutionary Poet Allen Ginsberg

Like Walt Whitman, poet Allen Ginsberg (1926 - 1997) was interested in writing that broke free of restraints, expressed the depths of the human soul and promoted an egalitarian outlook on life. Like Whitman, Ginsberg championed human rights. Whitman wrote often about America and about what it means to be American. Ginsberg wrote, "It occurs to me that I am America," identifying himself with the spirit of the nation.

Ginsberg was a member of the "beat generation" that was popularized in the 1950s with the publication of Jack Kerouac's renowned book, *On the Road*. The Beats strove to create literature that was similar to jazz music. It had a feel of improvisation and spontaneity. In 1955, Ginsberg read his book-length poem *Howl* in San Francisco. The book shocked the public and at the same ignited a generation. An obscenity charge against Ginsberg, who was gay, brought the book even greater publicity. You can find a copy of *Howl* on *poets.org*. Read it and get inspired to write a "howl" of your own.

Performance Poetry

In recent years a phenomenon has occurred in the world of poetry: Poetry Slams! Poets have always performed poetry. The poets who entertained people at feasts and festivals were once called "bards." But Slam Poetry has brought the idea of performance poetry to new levels with competitions that are held in nearly every major city.

Performance poetry does not follow the conventions of "academic poetry," which is one way to categorize the kinds of poems that are published in major literary magazines. It may not rely as heavily on imagery. It is usually not as nuanced and often blunter when it comes to meaning, but it has invigorated an entire generation of poets with its emphasis on rhythm, expression, and passion. Often it is profane, sometimes graphic, and almost always emotionally charged. You might think of performance poetry as standing somewhere between academic poetry and rap.

To fully "get" performance poetry, you have to hear it. Go to a live poetry slam or put the words "slam poetry" or "performance poetry" in your search engine and see what you can find. You will be surprised and moved.

Blog/Journal Assignment:

Read "Paul Revere's Ride" by Henry Wadsworth Longfellow. (It can be found online or in most libraries.) Then write your own ballad of about 12 to 16 lines. Don't worry if the meter or the rhyme isn't perfect, just see what you can come up with. Choose someone who has "legendary" status in your mind. This could be someone at your school, a superhero, or older brother or sister. You could even write it about yourself, creating your own legend.

Research Assignment:

Look up a contemporary poet with whom you are not yet familiar (Billy Collins, Nikki Giovanni, Lawrence Ferlinghetti, Yusef Komunyakaa, e.e. cummings, Sylvia Plath, John Ashberry, Robert Creeley, Louise Gluck, Ai, Rita Dove, Wanda Phipps, Amiri Baraka, Tai Li). Choose one poem that you find interesting in style. Write an homage poem by writing a poem that is similar in style and/or subject matter to the poem you have chosen. Print out both poems and bring them to your workshop or class to share.

Student Writing Samples

Student writer Grady Garrison wrote a sonnet about a person living with regrets.

Sonnet to a Life Not Lived

An old soul contemplates a withered tree
Its gnarls and branches weathered and askew.
For him it represents lost liberty;
Chance revoked, opportunity eschewed.

Memories of life bring smiles, wistfully
Though reflections of pain unearthed anew.
It has been too long since light met this tree
Like his memories of joy: too far, too few.

Solemnly, realization occurs,
He could have done more to nurture this life.
Softly weeping, his vision slowly blurs.
Maybe he'll do better in the afterlife.

Still he sits alone, longing for the past.
One last tear falls, for the life that has passed.

-- Grady Garrison

Here are some student Haikus:

Schism of experience
Dividing all of me now
Pushing my own envelope

-- Jack Straub

Eyes a pale blue
So cold and desolate, like
a remote iceberg

Shoes crush the gravel
Trees that tower over you
The air smells of pine

-- Alexander Murphy

Leaves changing color,
Creating new canvases
On which we paint life.

-- Grady Garrison

I like to read excerpts from "Howl" to my students and then ask them to write their own "howl." In this example, student writer Grady Garrison uses the repetition technique for his howl:

It's For Your Own Good

It's for your own good:
Create a world of privacy from each other,
Live fearfully in your neighborhood.

It's for your own good:
There are no secrets from us;
We know your lives, whether we can or should.

It's for your own good.

Yes we read your emails.
Yes we record your conversation.
How to know what that spam entails?
How to know terrorism from jubilation?

We do these things for you, don't you know?
Why do you need a vote to help your country's security grow?

You may call it secretive,
The way we furtively spy.
Instead of permission, forgive!
What's deemed necessary in our eyes.

-- Grady Garrison

D'Avva's "Howl" response reminds me of the great Maya Angelou or Lucille Clifton, but of course, it's got D'Avva's personal imprint.

Beauty, Manufactured for Skin Deep

I'm sorry, do I offend you? Do my curves, does my confidence, does my lack of damns about how you think I should be OFFEND you? Good! Feel the wrath of one who cares not for your Hollister, Fitch, and Eagle. Gaze at the glory who is one that does not worship at the feet of Victoria, Aerie, and Navy! I am stronger than your rail oppression, more beautiful than your rib rituals, more resilient than your adolescent mannequin!

I am flesh that covers the bone, pads the organs, entices the eye. While these thighs will never fit a size 2, they will certainly collect 2 to 5 sets of adoring eyes.

I am weary of the deflation, exploitation, and generalization of my fellow women. We are not dolls to be molded at the whim of the media, to be broken under the boot of society!!

My face is my own, no powders, oozes or smears. Do you know how disheartening it is to be told that "real" beauty does not exist when I utter that make up does not grace my already beautiful face? To be told that my beauty is impossible without brush, paste or tube?

So, I look you in the eye and I demand that you look me back in mine. For the girl who is hated because she cannot put on weight, the girl who is scared to apply food to her plate even as her belly brutally aches, for the girl who cries, hating herself, merely because she is a size 8, I look you in the eye and I demand that you look me back in mine. Do you really think we've come all that far?

-- D'Avva Holiday

Vocabulary

Define the following and add any other words that you have encountered recently:

Abolitionist

Ballad Meter

Couplet

Free Verse

Irony

Nuance

Open Form

Profane

Sloven

Volition

Writing Prompts

1. Sit outside and write three to five haiku poems about what you see, hear, and otherwise notice.

2. Write a love sonnet (or a hate sonnet!) You can model your sonnet after one of Shakespeare's if that helps you. You could write a sad sonnet in memory of someone who has died. Or a funny sonnet about something that happened to you. Make sure your sonnet is 14 lines long. Make sure there's a rhyme scheme.

3.   What makes you angry? What are your deepest beliefs? What would you like to change about the world? Maybe you have nothing to complain about. But take a look around. In our own communities, people go hungry. Around the world, children are dying of curable diseases. Powerful companies pollute our air and water. Find something to speak up about and do it in your very own "howl."

Unit Two

Scene

Chapter Seven
Seeing the Scene

One of the toughest concepts for beginning creative writers is grasping the importance of the scene. In fiction, creative nonfiction, and drama, especially, the scene is paramount. The scene is the method by which you allow your reader to inhabit your character's world. The scene is how you pull your reader into a situation and engage him emotionally. The scene is what makes writing come alive.

A scene is a rendering of an event that takes into account the setting, the action, and the words of one or more characters, as they would occur in "real time." Scenes are slow. The more action, then the slower they are. They show rather than tell.

Scenes are an important element of prose narrative, but in this unit we'll look at how scenes are used in drama, film, and television since these genres typically rely more obviously on scene to get the story across.

Drama as an Art Form

Drama embodies elements of different arts. Like fiction, drama is usually (but not always) based in narrative. Like poetry, drama makes use of language, timing and emotion. Like the visual arts, drama involves illusion and spectacle. Like dance, drama utilizes movement.

Drama is one of the oldest of the literary arts, developed by the ancient Greeks in the fifth century. The Greeks divided drama into two categories: tragedy and comedy. Today we define tragedy as a play or story with a sad ending (usually death) and comedy as a funny story with a happy ending (usually marriage). But in Ancient Greece, Aristotle defined tragedy as a drama that concerns people such as heroes, kings, or gods whose fortunes take a turn for the worse. For instance, Oedipus the king of Thebes learns that he has killed his father and married his own mother when his people are beset by a plague. Comedy, on the other hand, revolves around the fortunes of ordinary people whose luck changes from bad circumstances to better – an Adam Sandler movie, for example.

Over the centuries many forms of theatre have evolved including Elizabethan drama (Shakespeare and others), farce, melodrama, satire, theater of the absurd, historical plays, musicals, ten-minute plays, skits, and so on.

Contemporary Drama

Much of the drama during the second half of the 20th century was written to convey psychological realism. Plays such as *Who's Afraid of Virginia Woolf, Proof, Doubt, Long Day's Journey Into Night, The Glass Menagerie,* and *Death of a Salesman* captured and conveyed how and why people do the things they do. Although the goal was psychological realism, the means often included dream sequences, flashbacks, and symbolic characters.

Towards the end of the 20th century, playwrights began to experiment with new material, new techniques and new ways of telling stories. *Angels in America* by Tony Kushner is a great example of a play that tackles a tough subject for its time (the impact of AIDS) and uses an angelic figure to help tell the story. In the 1990sEve Ensler created a show called The *Vagina Monologues*, a series of monologues by different women, which has become a rallying cry against domestic violence.

Today playwrights and performers make drama in ever more creative ways. Improv groups, performance artists, circus acts, puppeteers, and avant-garde writers have stretched and expanded the definition of drama in new and exciting directions. One group of playwright-performers called The Neofuturists has created a series of two-minute plays that the actors perform in the order that the audience calls for. They placed numbered post cards on the stage, the audience calls out a number, and then the actors quickly grab their props and get into their roles. Sometimes the plays are silly. Sometimes they are heartbreaking.

What Makes a Play Great?

Drama involves the emotions: desire, fear, pity, love, hate, and so forth. But it must tell us something about those emotions. We must explore the motivations and consequences of the behaviors instigated by the emotions. A man standing on stage bellowing in rage might be entertaining for a few minutes, but after a while the audience will ask "why?" and what is he going to do about it.

The tragedy *Romeo and Juliet* by William Shakespeare begins with a deadly feud between two families, the Capulets and the Montagues. The first complication occurs when the Montagues' son, Romeo, and the Capulets' daughter, Juliet, meet at a party and fall in love. They feel that their love is bigger than the long-standing hatred between the two families, and they sneak off and marry. But when Romeo murders Juliet's cousin in revenge for the murder of his best friend, Romeo is banished. Then Juliet's parents try to force her to marry Count Paris. Adamant that she won't marry Paris, Juliet goes to her friend, the friar, and asks him what to do. He suggests that she fake her own death by taking a sleeping potion, which will fool her friends and family. Juliet takes the potion and now we have another complication. Everyone thinks she is dead. When Romeo finds Juliet in her tomb, he believes she is actually dead. In his grief he drinks poison and dies beside her. When Juliet awakens and finds Romeo dead, she plunges his dagger into her breast, preferring death to life without her love. Being a teenager has always been rough.

We can identify at least four elements that give this play its enduring popularity:

- Characters we care about (Romeo and Juliet)
- A plot with surprising complications (murders, mistakes, forced marriages, etc.)
- Emotional language (love and passion)
- A powerful premise (great love is more important than life itself)

Lajos Egri, author of *The Art of Dramatic Writing* says that the most important element of those listed above is a powerful premise. Without a strong premise, "the author's conviction is missing. Until he takes sides, there is no play. Only when he champions one side of the issue does the premise spring to life. Does egotism lead to loss of friends? Which side will you take? We, the readers or spectators of your play, do not necessarily agree with your conviction. Through your play you must therefore prove to us the validity of your contention." You might think of a play as an argumentative essay. It has a thesis and must prove it.

Egri provides a list of premises. Here are just a few of premises that Egri cites but they'll give you a good idea what he means:

- Foolish generosity leads to poverty.
- Honesty defeats duplicity.
- Heedlessness destroys friendship.
- Ill-temper leads to isolation.
- Bragging leads to humiliation.
- Dishonesty leads to exposure.
- Dissipation leads to self-destruction.
- Egotism leads to loss of friends.

Irony

Irony has several meanings. Usually, it means that something is not as it seems or that something doesn't happen the way we think it should.

Here are some examples of situational irony:

- Someone seems to be mean, but that person is the one who helps you when you need it the most.
- A soldier comes home safe from the war, but then gets killed in a car accident on the way home.
- A young woman pretends to be dead so that she can run away with her lover, but the lover believes she really is dead and so commits suicide.
- A man leaves home because of a prophecy that he will kill his father and marry his mother. He doesn't realize that he is really adopted. By fleeing to another land, he winds up killing his birth father and marrying his birth mother.

Dramatic irony refers to irony that is understood by the viewers but not the characters of a play.

Blog/Journal Assignment:

1. What plays or musicals have you seen? Have you ever been in a play? How is a play different from a movie or a novel?
2. Make a list of "lessons" you have learned in your life.

Research Assignment:

Go see a live play at some point during this unit on scene and write a 500-word paper discussing three or more of the following: premise, characters, action, comic or tragic elements, use of language, dramatic irony.

Vocabulary

Define the following and add any new words that you have encountered recently:

Dissipation

Farce

Melodrama

Premise

Satire

Student Writing Sample

Student writer Ashley Nichols wrote this scene that shows a couple at a crossroads.

The Letter

By Ashley Nichols

Setting: A kitchen with a breakfast area in an apartment. The kitchen has a counter and cabinets along the back wall. In the breakfast nook, there is only a kitchen table in view, with nothing but an opened letter sitting on it.

At Rise: JACE, 24, sits in one of the two chairs holding his head between his hands.

CLARISSA, 24, enters. She wears office clothes and carries a briefcase.

                    CLARISSA
Hey, I'm home.

(Jace looks up at her)

                    JACE
(In a defeated voice) Hey

                    CLARISSA
What's wrong? You don't sound so great.

                    JACE
Oh it's nothing, just work stuff. The usual stress. You know how that goes.

                    CLARISSA
Yeah, I know that one. Although I have some exciting news! I was going to call and tell you earlier, but I wanted to wait until I could tell you in person.

                    JACE
Oh, yeah? What happened?

                    CLARISSA
Remember how I was telling you that I was up for the management promotion at work, but I didn't think I was going to get it? We all thought Jackie was going to get it since she was always the favorite, but they surprised everyone and after two years of working my way up, I finally got it!

                    JACE
(halfheartedly) Oh that's great babe. I need to talk with you about something though

(Clarissa too excited to really notice the lack of excitement from Jace continues on.)

              CLARISSA
Okay, sure. But let's celebrate first! I just can't believe that all of that work finally paid off. I finally feel like I'm getting somewhere in my career and not just suffocating under piles of tedious paperwork and coffee errands.

              JACE
Yeah, I'm really proud of you…. I got a letter today.

              CLARISSA
Oh, yeah. I saw that on the table. Is it from your mom? I know she likes to send us letters sometimes. They're always so sweet.

(Clarissa opens one of the bags she brought in and removes two bottles of wine)

              CLARISSA
So I thought we should celebrate, and I bought two bottles of wine. One's that really great Moscato we liked last time, but I picked up a new Pinot Noir too, in case we wanted to try that.

              JACE
Either one. You pick. I'm not really in the mood for a drink.

              CLARISSA
Oh, come on. Well I'm going to pour myself a tall glass of Moscato. It's not every day you get promoted at work.

(Clarissa grabs a glass from the cabinet and pours herself a glass)

              CLARISSA
You know I thought you would be more excited for me.

              JACE
Clarissa, can you put the wine down and come sit over here.

(With a look of confusion and unease, Clarissa sets the glass of wine down on the counter. She slowly walks to the kitchen table and sits down in the chair opposite of Jace.)

              JACE
The letter is from the Marines. I hate to tell you this, but I'm getting restationed Clarissa. They're moving me to the base in Virginia, and I'm going to have to go on another tour.

(Clarissa is silent. Staring off into the distance with a stunned look on her face.)

            JACE

Clarissa, say something please.

            CLARISSA

(In a quiet voice still staring off into the distance) How soon?

            JACE

Next month

            CLARISSA

(Frantically) But I thought you weren't going on another tour. This is your last year. This was supposed to be a permanent home for us. I waited to start my career here. Why? Why now?

            JACE

With everything going on with ISIS in the Middle East, they're sending troops back in. I'm sorry Clarissa.

(Her head snaps to look at Jace)

            CLARISSA

But my life is here, your life is here. OUR life is here.

(Jace sighs in a defeated manner)

            JACE

I know....

(They both sit in silence while Clarissa stares into the distance and Jace searches her face for answers)

            CLARISSA

There's nothing for me in Virginia, Jace. Nowhere for me to pursue my career. I won't be successful there. It would be a death sentence to the career I'm trying to build and a funeral for the one I've started here. You know how bad I want this.

            JACE

I know, but I want you to come with me. I need you, Clarissa. I need you to be in Virginia with me until I leave. But I can't ask you to do that. I can't ask you to sacrifice even more for me. I'm sorry. I don't know what more to say than I'm sorry. There's no good way out this situation and I'm sorry.

            CLARISSA

I don't know, Jace. I don't know what to say.

                    JACE
Say you'll come with me.

                  CLARISSA
I don't know, Jace. I don't know.

Writing Prompts

1. Make a list of ten "lessons" you have learned from your life.

2. Write about an ironic situation from your own life. This might be a time when someone acted in a way that was surprising to you. Or it could be a time when things didn't turn out the way you expected them to turn out.

Chapter Eight
Solo Acts: Writing the Monologue

The word "mono" means "one," and "logo" means "word" or "voice." A dialogue involves speech between two or more characters whereas a monologue is spoken by one character. If you've ever watched a talk show on late night television, then you're familiar with a common type of monologue. The hosts usually begin the show telling jokes and funny stories directly to the audience. This is called a monologue.

Dramatic Monologues

In theatre, a monologue can be a long speech from one character to another. Or it can be a long speech that the character makes to a group of characters or to the audience. For example, in the play "Proof," which was also made into a movie, the main character stands up at her father's wake and gives a speech to the people who are at the wake honoring her father, the same people who ignored him for the last five years of his life when he was suffering from dementia.

Another example of a monologue is the speech that Mark Antony gives in Shakespeare's play *Julius Caesar*, which begins with those immortal words, "Friends, Romans, countrymen, lend me your ears . . ."

Here is the beginning of Mark Antony's long monologue. Do you catch the irony?

> *I come to bury Caesar, not to praise him;*
> *The evil that men do lives after them,*
> *The good is oft interred with their bones,*
> *So let it be with Caesar ... The noble Brutus*
> *Hath told you Caesar was ambitious:*
> *If it were so, it was a grievous fault,*
> *And grievously hath Caesar answered it ...*
> *Here, under leave of Brutus and the rest,*
> *(For Brutus is an honourable man;*
> *So are they all; all honourable men)*
> *Come I to speak in Caesar's funeral ...*
> *He was my friend, faithful and just to me:*
> *But Brutus says he was ambitious;*

And Brutus is an honourable man....
He hath brought many captives home to Rome,
Whose ransoms did the general coffers fill:
Did this in Caesar seem ambitious?
When that the poor have cried, Caesar hath wept:
Ambition should be made of sterner stuff:

Stand-Alone Monologues

An entire performance may be comprised of a long monologue. Stand-up comedians often tell jokes within the context of a monologue. This can be a short routine such as you might see on the "Tonight Show" or a long one such as the routines of Louis C.K. Some performance artists such as Anna Deavere Smith have made a career out of delivering monologues from a variety of characters, as she did in her play *Twilight: Los Angeles 1992* about the 1992 Los Angeles riots. Spalding Gray wrote a long monologue that was eventually made into the movie *Swimming to Cambodia*.

However, most monologues are much shorter than a full-length play. Typical monologues run between two and five minutes.

Writing Monologues

Actors often use monologues (either from plays or as stand-alones) as audition pieces to display their talents. Actors are always in need of fresh, well-written monologues.

The monologue performer may be playing himself or herself or may adopt a persona. A monologue usually tells a story, which revolves around an event or an emotional development or both. Even in a short monologue, there is a sense of a beginning, middle, and end. (Performance poetry has much in common with the monologue.)

Writing a monologue helps you get to know your character. Through monologues we learn who a character is, what he or she thinks about and what are the circumstances that he or she currently faces. As you write your monologues, identify the experiences this character has had that inform her or his behavior now. Ask yourself, what emotional responses are appropriate for her or him. Then capture the character's voice by using idiolect or particular words and phrases that individualize the character.

Remember there is more to a monologue than just words—they come to life in performance. There must be emotional content to engage the audience and the actor. The performer of the monologue whether yourself or an actor needs to feel that there is enough to fully inhabit this character, not just through the words but through body language and tone as well.

As with poetry and prose writing, you can find material for monologues from your own life. Or you can research historic events or current topics to find material. Your monologue may be in your voice or you may create a fictional character.

Some tips for writing your monologue:

- Skip the exposition and jump right into the middle of the problem. You might even start towards the end of the event you are describing and fill in details as you go along.

- Be purposeful. The monologue is not just a random moment from a character's life. It happens at a crucial, specific time. What is it that this character absolutely has to say right now? What does he or she need to tell us?

- Be sure that you know this character well – her hopes, fears and ambitions. What does she want more than anything else?

- Convey this character to us through authentic language, known as vernacular. Let your character speak with vocabulary, diction and phraseology that would be natural. Listen to how people speak and then exaggerate.

- Read your work aloud to make sure you have the right cadence. Like poetry, a monologue relies on sound for much of its power.

- Make every word count. As with poetry, a monologue packs a lot of information into a small format.

- Pay attention to the structure of your monologue. Let the tension build up to a climax and then release it at the end. Often the ending will be a reflection of the first few lines, clarifying them or amplifying them.

The Soliloquy

A soliloquy is a moment of "interior monologue," (which you will study in the next unit) but because the audience is not made up of mind readers, the characters must speak their thoughts as though the drama had a cinematic voiceover.

The most famous soliloquy, of course, belongs to young Hamlet in the eponymous play by William Shakespeare, which begins with the memorable line: _____.

Research Assignment:

Go online and watch two different versions of Hamlet's soliloquy. What are the differences? What is the emotional import of the soliloquy? Jot down some notes for class discussion.

Blog Assignment:

Go through your photos. Find a picture that brings back memories. Tell the story of that picture, that day, that moment in a monologue.

Student Writing Samples:

In this first sample, Stefond takes on the persona of one of the elder women in his family. Notice the conversational tone.

Christmas Monologue

Hey, Mary Alice, and Merry Christmas to you. Oh, we had a lovely dinner today. You know all my grandbabies were in town and my kids. Everybody came over and Stephanie, child, oh Stephanie just brought me the prettiest table cloth you ever seen in yo' life, girl. Yes, she did. I knew I raised that one right. Me, Stephanie and Lila made some great food. We had a ham and a roast. The kids wanted to help so we let them make some baked beans. Oh, girl, nobody ate them thangs cause they was so burnt. We made some macaroni and cheese, some tata salad, cole slaw, everything was just so beautiful, so beautiful. You know the men. Don't wanna do nothin' in the kitchen, but as soon as they smell somethin' wanna come runnin' and askin' when it's gon' be done. I told 'em to go back in there and watch some TV and that was the end of that. Oh, gurl, I just remembered Bo knocked over the damn gravy boat and got gravy all over the table cloth and I think he 'bout finished the table that old rickety table been in our family since, since older than me. But yeah, we had a good day, a good Christmas. What about yours?

-- Stefond Johnson

Deanna wrote this monologue from the point of view of herself.

The Rules of the Table

My family isn't all that large but we're all very close and y'know every family has their traditions and things they pass off from generation to generation so my family's no exception. Our biggest tradition you could say the one that's the most important to us has to do with Thanksgiving and Christmas dinner. There's a certain etiquette, well kind of more like a routine… no, it's like a set of rules on how you eat dinner. First off, you have to say grace with the family before you even serve the food. That's rule number one. You have to stand in a circle around the food so that the prayer is locked into the table and no matter how rough or sweaty the person next to you's hands are, you have to hold on or the prayer will break free or fly away or something. Second, whenever you're ready to serve yourself, whoever actually finds the plates first gets served first and the line must form behind them. No cutsies just because your mouth is watering and slobber is dripping to the floor. The third and probably most important rule is that your food must coordinate. If you get turkey, you have to get gravy, no matter how thin or watered down it is. Ham is salty so you have to get a roll and/or salad with it. And my family's Jamaican so if you get curry goat you have to get rice and peas. Y'know, given. No excuses. There's no "It's too spicy" or "It's too dry" or "I don't like it." You might as well say "I want out of this family." And even if you really do want out of the family, that's rule number four: No one gets out alive.

-- Deanna Denham

Monologues often come from strong emotions. Here's a monologue that expresses a rejected lover's rage:

I've written a thousand words to you. I've given my feelings towards you more life via these 26 letters than some people have given words life in their life times. Three years. Three years of ups, downs, sideways, no ways, all things that exist that make people believe and forget and love and hate. I have given you more than a thousand words. I have written to you with blood and let your existence sink into my bones. I have given you my very soul, let you touch me in ways that no one had ever touched before. I was pure! Pure enough to feel like I was something close to whole and even when the dark spots showed on my flawless visage, you cupped them and embraced them with the delicate fingertips that only a lover knows how to use. I gave in to you. I surrendered something that I didn't know meant so much to me, but I know now why it was so important. I was, No dammit I AM in love. I am in love from the looseness of my head curls to the tightness of my toes curling, I am in love with the very breath you inhale, exhale, inhale, exhale, inhale me back into your arms where my heart has been beating all along. I am no longer whole! YOU TOOK MY VERY SOUL. I didn't know I could write sonnets across the inside of your brain, but I did. With my fingertips, with my tongue, with my legs, arms, back, neck, palms, I wrote you a thousand and more words! I exist as a shell that shields me from life because I am hollow. There is no one home here. I am alone here. You took with you something that I didn't know was there. You snatched it like a greedy child just as it was about to bloom. I am alone inside this place, this shell. You told me you wanted me to share, well where do my emotions go? Gales of depression rain shards of ice into my flesh, volcanic eruptions of anger boil me to my bones. I am a mass of things come unglued and all I want is to hate you. I should hate you, should loathe your very existence, but I do not, CANNOT, undo this. Only you can. Was it something I said? Does she make you happier? Am I just a burden? Does the freedom make you feel free, or was I just the only problem? I once read a poem you wrote. I've hidden it away now, but it was so painful to hear the same voice throw me out the door. Take the shirts, the dresses, the bears and the blankets. Take the kisses, the hugs, the lust, and the laughter. Take it all with you if you are so determined to leave me here. I'd rather keep my scars and pick them anew knowing that "one day" will never come. Leave me to bleed, leave me to rot, leave me to slowly melt away into the nothingness, but don't you dare tell me you love me, don't you dare tell me you have "feelings" don't you DARE tell me that you miss me when I apologize and try to rectify and then you look me in the eye and tell me it's not enough.

-- D'Avva Holiday

Vocabulary

Define the following and add any new words that you have encountered recently:

Eponymous

Soliloquy

Topical

Vernacular

Writing Prompts

1. What are family holiday dinners like in your house? What are the traditions, the foods, the family squabbles? Tell us about it. You may speak as yourself or you may choose to write in the voice of someone else in the family.

2.   Other ideas for monologues

- a crush that wasn't reciprocated
- a journal entry from the past
- a time when you felt jealousy, guilt, or desire
- an important phone conversation
- a painful or joyous memory
- a moment of forgiveness or redemption
- an event in the news that ignites emotions

Chapter Nine
Character and Motivation

When you wrote your monologue, you were creating a character -- even if that character was based on you. The truth is that even the most autobiographical writers must choose pieces of themselves for their writing. They can't show the whole person because it would take too long and be too complicated. An interesting character is not just one-dimensional, however. A main character, especially, will have strengths and weaknesses, good qualities and bad qualities, courage and fear.

Creating a character that is like ourselves can be effective because we know what we think and feel and move through the world. Often we'll go back to a younger version of ourselves. Then we can change the name, the physical description, even the gender. I wrote a story about something that happened to me when I was seven. I made the character a boy named Joey and I gave him a little sister. But Joey is still me in many ways.

Experienced writers will tell you that there is a little bit of themselves in all their characters, even the villains. When creating a character from that personal seed, writers can then change details such as age, background, physical appearance, gender. When you start changing the details, you'll notice that even though the character is similar to you, that character will begin to take on a life of her or his own.

Developing Characters

As you probably know there are major characters and minor characters. We won't worry about minor characters here. They rarely need development. But your main character, or your protagonist, needs to have certain elements in order for your audience to believe in him or her.

- A goal -- What does your main character want? What is standing in her way? What character traits will enable her to get what she wants or prevent her from doing so?
- A fear or a flaw -- What is your main character's weakness? What is he afraid of?
- A back-story -- What has happened to your character to mold her? You may borrow details from your own life, from a friend's life, from stories you've heard about people and/or make them up. Sometimes we create a back story from a combination of the above. Think about what has happened to your character in the past. This will likely inform how the character feels about present circumstances.

- Change -- How will your character change over the course of the story? This is called the character arc.

In many dramas the protagonist must deal with an antagonist (or villain). The antagonist will have many of the same features as the protagonist: a goal, usually the opposite of the protagonist's goal, a fear, and a back-story. The most interesting antagonists will not be pure evil. They will usually have more bad qualities than good, and sometimes they will be working with good intentions but have a skewed or ineffective view of how the world works—but no matter your antagonist's background and intentions, the most important thing is that they are intriguing to your reader. Sometimes the antagonist will change over the course of the story, but oftentimes it just doesn't matter. We're more concerned with change in the protagonist.

Can there be more than one protagonist? Of course. Generally, however, your audience will want to identify (and root for) one or two characters.

Seed Ideas

Writers get their ideas for drama from their own lives, from stories in the news, and from things that happen to other people. Writers also like to play a game called "what if?" What if I were on an island with a nutcase who liked to hunt people? What if I were stranded on an island in the ocean and there were cannibals out to get me? What if people thought I was dead and I had the chance to float down the Mississippi on a raft with a runaway slave? What if I owned a time machine? Daydreaming is part of the writer's job. That's how great plots are born.

It's important that the seed idea have some emotional value and that it be based in the existential experience of a character. The idea "stopping war" may be noble, but it's not that interesting. On the other hand, a play about some women who are sick of their husbands being gone all the time (the existential situation) and decide to stop war by denying sex to their husbands could turn out to be a great idea because your audience will be just as interested in the women who hatch this scheme as they are in the theme or message of the story.

It is often a useful approach to consider the circumstances and existential condition of your characters, and then to let their movement through the world generate the plot, instead of conceiving the plot and then forcing your characters to walk through it like a labyrinth. Of course, maybe you want to tell a story about a character who is trapped in the plot and needs to escape—like Robert Ludlum's spy thrillers—in which case devising the plot first could be useful. Consider your goals and then decide your approach, but whatever approach you take, remember:

Motivated Characters Move the Plot

Characters are motivated by their situations, their dreams, and their fears. It may be that the character doesn't realize she is in trouble, but the reader should know early on that there is a problem to be solved. Otherwise, readers or viewers simply won't sign up for the ride. Imagine going to a theme park and taking a trolley ride around the parking lot. Not much to see. The cars are nicely parked. The trolley ride is smooth, but this is not the part of your vacation that you'll describe on the postcards to friends back home. Once you get inside the park, you'll pay good money to go on a roller coaster, a haunted house tour or some ride that throws you up, down and sideways. You want scary things to jump out and make you scream. That's what you pay the money for, not the nice trolley ride around the parking lot.

The character's motivation drives the plot. Plot comes from the conflicts and tensions that are the bones of the story. Conflict produces tension, which is created by two forces opposing each other. Conflict is when you want to go out with your friends, and your parents say you have to go to a family function instead. Tension is the feeling in the car as you drive past your friends having fun while you are on your way to go to the awful family function.

Types of conflicts include:

- The protagonist against another individual
- The protagonist against nature (or technology)
- The protagonist against society
- The protagonist against God
- The protagonist against himself or herself

The plot can be charted by "plot points." Each thing that happens to complicate the story is a plot point. The climax is the turning point of the story – the moment when the outcome of the story will be decided.

When we talk about the plot of a story, we mean a sequence of causally related events (one thing causes another to happen which causes something else). A plot usually begins with an inciting incident: something happens to get the ball rolling. In *Oedipus Rex*, the inciting incident is a plague that afflicts the people of Thebes. The inciting incident causes something to happen, i.e. Oedipus sends Creon to find out from the Oracle why the citizens are suffering from this plague. It also causes Oedipus to question the blind seer about his origins. Each succeeding thing that happens (plot point) causes something else to happen until in the end, Oedipus blinds himself at the climax and is driven out of Thebes.

Low-key Plots

Sometimes inexperienced writers believe that plot means car chases, thousands of dead bodies, and nuclear explosions. It's true that these big plots can be spectacular. However, for learning purposes, it will probably be more helpful to concentrate on conflicts that are closer to your realm of experience.

Earlier we talked about a character having a goal. This goal can be as simple as a young man wanting to get to know a young woman. But then for this to be an interesting drama, there has to be some conflict:

- She has a jealous boyfriend. (person versus person)
- He is terribly shy. (person versus self)
- She is rich and he is poor. (person versus society)
- A hurricane hits the town where they live. (person versus nature)

Research Assignment:

Go on line and look up Freytag's Triangle. Be ready to discuss with your class or writing group.

Blog Assignment:

Make a list of some conflicts you have experienced in the past.

Student Writing Sample

Writer's Block

by D'Avva Holiday

Characters:

Lucian: aloof, gentle, caring, poetic

Stephan: self-doubting, strong willed, determined, crafty

Setting: A grassy field during the mid-afternoon. In the distance, the edges of a playground can be seen, but no one upon it. Trees dot the area, usually in clusters, and line a path that is off to the right of the characters and seems to lead towards the playground.

(Stephen is sitting on the ground, slightly reclined, and staring up into the sky.)

Stephan
Even if I didn't come before you, you died out long before I did.

Lucian
I am but a cloud, drifting over a summer day. I may linger over one spot, casting shadow on everything that lies beneath, or I may race past, shielding all from the light for just a moment so that it might catch its breath

Stephan
You speak in riddles and stanzas. Why can't you speak plainly?

Lucian
I also speak in tongues. Care to test me on that?

Stephan
Did you just hit on me??

Lucian
I do not recall rising from my spot nor do I remember swinging any of my limbs. Do you see bruises or feel pain?

Stephan
When was the last time she's even written about you? How are you not coated in dust?

(Lucian rolls onto back and wiggles arms in the air.)

Lucian
I drift in and out, shifting forms from fog to crystalline clarity

Stephan
(Sighing)

When was the last time she wrote about me? Will she ever finish my story? I was to be a king, a ruler! I was destined to be a legend! My tale...why does she leave it unwritten?

(Lucian gracefully sits up and then with the ease and speed of a cat rises from the ground)

Lucian
She dreams up your life, she just never has time to get you to the paper or the words disappear when she does. She is a dreamer...a beautiful dreamer who gets lost in her own dreams and imaginations.

(Spotlight on Lucian grows smaller.)

Stephan
Where are you going? Don't start to fade away! I was just starting to get curious. Do you remember your old lives?

Lucian
I am eternal, my life going in a seamless circle of recycling. If I should die, from my ashes someone new will be reborn. Tis' neither painful nor harmful, just something we forgotten ones do.

(Lucian slowly walks backwards, the spotlight growing smaller.)

Stephan
You don't have to fade...You can fight this!

Lucian
Does the fairy live if no one believes in her? Do the gods not lose strength if no one worships at their alters? Does the imagination not wither and die when locked away from sight and use?

(Lucian offers a final smile before fading complete away. Stephan stares at the space where Lucian was.)

Stephan
...so how long before I begin doing the same?

Vocabulary

Define the following and add any other words that you have encountered recently:

Character arc

Existential situation

Freytag's triangle

Inciting incident

Writing Prompts

1. **Finding the Voice** - Make a list of eight to ten different "selves" you carry around with you. Choose one of those selves and let it tell its story.

2. Take one of the conflicts you identified in your blog and turn it into a short scene.

Chapter Ten
Dialogue: Conversations that Work

You are familiar with dialogue because you've been exposed to it in movies and television shows since you were a small child. And, in fact, whenever you have a conversation with another person, you are engaging in dialogue. Dialogue is an essential component of both drama and fiction, but dialogue is especially important in drama. When the curtain opens or the characters walk onto the set, the words they say will determine whether or not the audience is going to pay attention or start thinking about where they're going to eat after the show. It can keep them in their seats or send them sneaking off to the nearest exit.

In our everyday conversations, we waste a lot of words, but the rules are different for characters in drama. They must make their words pay.

Dialogue should do the following:

1.   Engage the audience's attention -- The dialogue sets up questions in the audience's minds. Why is this person upset? What is that person hiding? About whom are the characters talking?
3.   Reveal character -- The dialogue lets the audience know about the attitudes, background, education, concerns, and values of the characters.
4.   Propel the plot forward -- The truths that the characters reveal, the lies they tell, the yearning they express all move the plot forward. When Romeo tells Juliet that he wants to marry her, his words start a chain reaction that ends with their deaths.
5.   Explain the situation without "explaining" -- Dialogue for the stage must sound like real speech and yet must also be different from real speech. In expository writing (the type of writing you generally do for school or informative articles), you are used to explaining things. Dramatic dialogue needs to let the audience know what's going on without being obvious about it.

For example, let's say we have two characters on their way to the funeral of their mother. You wouldn't have one of your characters say, "I can't believe Mom died last night of pneumonia after battling cancer for the past three months." It would be ridiculously obvious that the dialogue's only purpose was to inform the audience what happened. Instead, you would use the give and take, the back and forth quality of dialogue to get your information across:

        Sandy

I can't believe she's gone.

        Joan

Me either.

(They silently pack belongings into boxes)

        Sandy

It's for the best, I guess.

        Joan

Maybe. I thought we'd have more time with her though. The doctors said she'd have six months. But it wasn't six months. It wasn't even three months. They lied to us, Sandy.

        Sandy

They didn't know she was going to get pneumonia. How could they have known?

In the example scene, the information isn't spoon-fed to the audience. The audience needs to pay attention and pick up clues. The developed scene also gives us some information about the emotional states of the two characters through their dialogue. Notice how the tension creates a more interesting scenario.

Techniques for Creating Dynamic Dialogue

Dynamic dialogue is dialogue with energy and power. It gets the play up and running. Here are a few guidelines for creating dynamic dialogue:

1. Let each main character have a particular way of speaking that reveals something about them. Perhaps one character flits around from subject to subject. Another one might be obsessive about something. Give one of your characters a particular idiolect, a few pet phrases or words. Be sure that we can differentiate your characters by the way they speak to one another.

2. Keep the language clear and concise. You may have a character that is a "real talker," but if that character takes over the play and doesn't get to the point, your audience is going to lose interest. So have the characters speak about interesting things. Have them talk about things that matter — or at least things that matter to them.

3. Tension is key. Find the underlying tension in the relationships of the characters. Who has the upper hand in the relationship? Sometimes the tension is created by the subtext: what the characters are not saying. What does each character want and how do the other characters help or hinder them?

4.   Make sure the dialogue is going somewhere. A change or revelation should happen through what is said or unsaid.

Note: Sometimes writers want to be directors and actors, too, but it usually doesn't work out that way. Once you've written your dialogue, it's up to the actor to interpret how to say it with perhaps some input from a director. But it is permissible to give a little guidance, especially if the way a piece of dialogue is said is crucial to its meaning. If the actor won't be able to tell how the line should be said from the context, then you may add in dialogue directions in parentheses.

> *Tom*
> *(angrily)*
> *No, I won't do it.*
> *Tammy*
> *(whispering)*
> *But you have to. If you don't, they'll kill you.*

Research Assignment:

Go to Google Books and read the first three pages (5, 6 and 7) of Beth Henley's play Crimes of the Heart. You'll see how the situation is explained through dialogue. Did you notice that you learned a lot about the characters (even the ones who weren't there) in just those few pages? Also, you may have noticed that the writer planted a mystery within the first few lines of dialogue: What is in the newspapers that is so awful? Later, we'll learn that the character Babe has shot her husband.

Blog Assignment:

Go to a mall, coffee shop, cafeteria, or any public place and pay attention to the way that people speak. Jot down phrases and words that help reveal character. For instance, an older person might say, "Pass the sugar, dear." A harried mom might say, "Get over here right this instance, buster!" A teenager might use text speak and say, "IDK." Find phrases that reveal age, gender, and general attitudes. Then write a short dialogue of one to three pages using some of the phrases and words you've heard.

Student Writing Sample

Following is a short skit written by two student writers in a collaborative exercise. It's a good example of creating a low-key plot and revealing character through dialogue and action. Plus, you can tell they had fun writing it.

Time to Say Goodbye

By Natalie Popovich and Stefond Johnson

Characters:

Boy, carrying a duffle bag.

Girl, boy's fiancée.

Announcer

Setting: An airport gate.

Announcer
Flight 6687 to New York will be boarding in five minutes.

Boy
We're here. Time to say goodbye.

Girl
No, not yet. Just hold me a little longer.

(They embrace)

Boy
Stop, you're, uh, going to make me cry.

(He begins to tear up)

Girl
Don't cry. Please, you'll make me cry too. Then we'll just be two sobbing fools.

(They both chuckle. Boy wipes his eyes.)

Boy
Yeah, I guess you're right. I just want to let you know that if I don't come back, I love you.

(Girl covers his mouth.)

Girl
Don't talk like that! You know you'll be fine... you'll be fine.

>   *Boy*
Can you take your hand off my mouth now?

>   *Girl*
Oh, yeah, I'm sorry.

(Girl takes her hand off his mouth. Long, awkward, silence)

>   *Boy*
You'll miss me, right?

>   *Girl*
I'll miss you when I walk through the park, when I pass by the tree that you carved our initials in. Or whenever I eat cauliflower ...

>   *Boy*
That's right. On our first date when I made you laugh so hard that you spit cauliflower on my face. I'll think of you every time I pass a door, remembering the countless times you ran into them.

>   *Girl*
Yes, I still feel the pain. And I'll think of you every time I'm on a roller coaster, after that one time, on the pony express... when you threw up... on my lap.

>   *Boy*
I'll think of that one time at band camp when you took my flute, and never gave it back.

>   *Girl*
I still have it, and I play it every night.

>   *Boy*
Well, I'm glad you still play with it. Do you think of me when you do it?

>   *Girl*
Every time. And I'll think of you when I go to church, after that one time you let one rip in service.

>   *Boy*
The Holy Spirit went through my small intestine that Sunday.

>   *Girl*
Amen!

>   *Boy*
But still, will you miss me?

>   *Girl*
Of course I will. That was a stupid question.

(Another boy walks past them.)

>   *Girl*
> Woo-woo, hey baby! *(Turns to boy) Yeah, I'll miss you.*

>   *Boy*
> *Man, it's time to say goodbye.*

> *(He walks offstage.)*

>   *Girl*
> *Was it something I said?*

> *(She shrugs and follows second boy offstage.)*

--Stefond Johnson and Natalie Popovich

Vocabulary

Define the following and add any new words that you have encountered recently:

concise

subtext

Writing Prompt

Choose one pair of characters from the following:

- Two siblings
- A man and a woman who are strangers
- A boyfriend and girlfriend
- Two football players
- Two rivals on a tennis team
- Two co-workers
- Two mothers
- Two fathers
- A doctor and her patient

Choose one setting

- a drugstore
- an office
- outside a school principal's office
- a field
- a kitchen
- a bus
- a back porch
- a hospital lobby
- a golf course

Now put your two characters into the setting you've chosen. You might let one character know something that the other one doesn't or one character has something that the other wants. You also might want to consider choosing a setting that is unexpected given the relationship of the characters—perhaps the doctor and her patient will meet by chance in a field. This strange meeting will perhaps encourage something strange and interesting to happen. Write for ten minutes and see what happens. This can be a collaborative exercise.

Chapter Eleven
Writing the Short Play

Now, it's time for you to write a short play. You may be familiar with this form from watching skits performed on television shows such as *Saturday Night Live*. Skits are short, funny scenes that could be loosely said to have a beginning, middle, and end.

As you write your play, remember that in drama you must show information through dialogue and action. We went over this in the previous chapter, but sometimes writers forget this important distinction when writing drama. In stage directions the inexperienced writer might write something like this: "Sean enters the room. He is upset because he has been fired from his job." The problem is that the audience doesn't get to read the stage directions, so they don't know what is going on with Sean. In the example below, the writer shows that Sean lost his job through his actions. He can also talk about losing his job or he can cover it up.

Example:

(Sean enters the room, carrying a box. He drops the box on the floor; papers and other office supplies fall out. He kicks the box and hurts his foot. Then he sits down with a dejected expression.)

(The phone rings. Sean answers.)

>   Sean
> *Hi, Mom. . . . Yeah. I'm fine, fine. . . Oh, work is great. Just great. Couldn't be better.*

(He picks up the stapler that has fallen out of the box and then drops it.)

>   Sean
> *Okay, Mom. See ya' later.*

(He hangs up the phone and groans.)

The Topic

You may already have an idea what to write about. You might have thought of a good premise and have some intriguing characters in mind. But if you're still wondering what to write about or if you want to sharpen the premise you've already got, think about what it is that you believe to be true about life. What are some things about which you feel strongly? Do you think that honesty is not always the best policy? Do you think that friendship should count more than romantic relationships? Do you believe that people should care about animals? Use your passion to fuel your creativity.

Format

One thing we haven't discussed is professional playwriting format. Here are a few guidelines you should follow:

- use 12-point Times New Roman font
- include no more than one paragraph of opening stage directions
- use single-space type
- double space for every new element, i.e. new character speaking
- put stage directions in parentheses

You can find many examples of proper play writing format online.

Getting Started

Here are some steps for getting started:

1. Begin your play *in media res*. You may take the scenes you've already written if you wish. Is there some crucial moment of tension that can get you jump-started? You don't need to spend a lot of time explaining how the characters got into the situation. Just show them in the situation and then work on resolving it.
2. Have your characters doing something—not just talking. For instance, they could be cooking, painting a house, fixing a car engine, burying a dead dog, playing a golf game. Give them some action.
3. Your dialogue needs to convey information either about the situation or about the characters themselves.
4. Either have your main character change in some way by the end OR allow the action to reveal something to your audience that they didn't know about the characters by the end.
5. Give each character a distinctive way of speaking. For instance, does he say "like" every other word? Does she use a lot of big words? Is he always cracking jokes? Don't be afraid to use repetition, rhythm, alliteration. Have fun with the language.

For a short play, you'll need to limit the scope of your work. That means one to three scenes with two to four characters. It also means *don't try to cover years or deal with huge historic events*. Let it be about the small but important moments in a person's life.

Don't worry if your play is not perfect. Writing is a process. Sometimes a piece of writing comes easily, but often it is difficult and may take many, many drafts.

As you begin to think about writing the short play, consider these questions:

- What is the premise that drives your play?
- What is the motivation that makes your characters act the way they do?
- What is the overriding emotion?
- Who are the characters? What are their goals?
- What are the conflicts?

Checklist

Once you've gotten a draft of your play written, read it over to see if it's got the following elements:

- Believable, interesting characters – Your characters may be quirky or eccentric, but we should still be able to believe they are based in reality. Is your main character complex – not all good or all bad?
- A Theme or Premise – What is the one sentence you can come up with that tells us what this play is about. For example, "betraying your friends will only leave you friendless" or "wars leave scars that never heal." Remember this should be a sentence, not a one-word topic.
- Conflict – What obstacles is your protagonist facing? Who is your antagonist? What is the problem?
- Suspense – What questions will your audience have at the beginning of the play that keep them watching till the end of the play?
- Lastly, ask yourself if you've written a play that will make people think.

Blog Assignment:

Make a list of ten things you strongly believe. Even if you don't use them for this play, you might use them for future work.

Research Assignment:

Read the interview on the PBS website with playwright Suzan-Lori Parks, who wrote the play "Topdog/Underdog." http://www.pbs.org/newshour/conversation/jan-june02/parks_4-11.html.

What did you learn about playwriting from the interview? If this interview is unavailable, use your search engine to find another one.

Writing Assignment:

Write your short play. It should be between five and ten pages long. You should have no more than four characters and no more than three settings. Try not to set your play in a car or have long scenes on telephones.

Student Writing Sample

This is the first scene from a short play about fictional characters.

Time and Time Again

By Rebecca Fisher

Characters:
Sylvia: crazy, smart, cunning, resourceful
Nurse: rude, short tempered, dumb, punctual
Setting: a room in a mental hospital
(A harried young woman paces back and forth in a room, empty except for one bed, with sterile fluorescent lighting. She wrings her hands continuously and glances at a clock on the wall. The clock has no hands.)

>   *Sylvia*
(Anxiously)
There it is again…My devil's metronome… tick tick tick. God do you hear that? That ticking sound… I hear it every moment of every day counting out seconds into minutes into hours never ceasing until I close my eyes and let it disappear but then there it is again jarring me from sleep it's back growing louder and more insistent. Tick tick ticking… A three armed monster dictating my world cutting me off from what I need. God, do you hear that? It's in my head my hands my feet. It's rocking me. I am vibrating with its impatience and every second I hear it mocking me. God, can you hear that sound?

(Three knocks on the door. Sylvia jumps and turns to see a young male nurse with a tray of tiny plastic cups. He smiles sadly at her.)

>   *Nurse*
It's that time again, Sylvia.

(She shakes her head backing away from him as he selects a cup from the tray.)

>   *Sylvia*
(Shouting)
Don't say that word!

            Nurse
Sylvia, I don't have time for this. Just take your pills.

            Sylvia
Don't say it!

(Sylvia takes the cup and puts the pills in her mouth rolling them around and making faces. Sylvia smacks her head repeatedly as if each impact will silence the ticking.)

            Nurse
That's it, take your time.

(Sylvia lunges forward knocking the tray from his hands spilling pills and cups everywhere each making a distinct sound. She sinks to the floor hands over her ears rocking back and forth. Then she reaches for something under the bed.)

            Nurse
You do this every time, Sylvia.

            Sylvia
Don't say that word.

            Nurse
(frustrated, staccato)
Time. Time. Time. It's a common word Sylvia. Get used to it.

(Sylvia stands slowly, turning something in her hand. She raises it high over her head and lunges forward again piercing the nurse's chest with the sharpened hand of a clock.)

            Sylvia
(shaking her head)
I told you time and time again, but you didn't listen.

Chapter Twelve
Writing the Video Scene

You've already written a play so you know some of the important elements that are required in dramatic writing. Screenwriting is another form of dramatic writing.

For your film scene, you will need to create:

- characters
- setting
- scenes
- conflict and tension
- emotion
- thematic purpose or premise

The difference now is that you have a little more freedom and can rely less on dialogue and more on images to get your point across.

As with theater, film is a collaborative art. The director, actors, editor, art directors and other members of the crew will interpret your story in their own way when it is filmed – unless, of course, you decide to make the film yourself.

Conventions of the Hollywood Script

Screenplays have a specific format, and screenwriters often use special software to help them meet the requirements. Because you probably don't have access to screenwriting software, we'll just go over a few of those requirements in this lesson. You can write your short video scene using these conventions if they apply.

The first thing your director needs to know about a scene is whether it is taking place indoors or outdoors and what time of day it is. The director needs to know this in order to secure a location and tell the lighting crew how to light the scene.

Each new scene starts with this information:

    INT. MIKE'S LIVING ROOM – DAY (or "EXT. _____")

That means the scene is an interior scene that takes place in Mike's living room and it is day.

The first two words of the script after the title are: FADE IN. Then you describe what the camera "sees". Usually the first shot is an "establishing" shot. It establishes where we are.

Example: The sun shines on a quiet street in a suburban neighborhood in front of a large red brick house.

To write a full-length screenplay requires more time and information than you can get in an introductory course, but if you want to learn more there are many resources on the Internet. If you want to learn the "lingo" of the screenwriting world, the glossary at this website may be helpful: http://www.screenwriting.info/glossary.php#spec-script. If you want to learn the rules of writing a full-length script, visit this website: http://www.screenwriting.info/

When you're writing your short screenplay, don't forget that film is visual. You must include what your viewers will see and hear. Unlike fiction, there is usually no room for interior monologue so you must show what they are thinking and feeling through their actions and dialogue. You do not need to include the types of shots (close up, long shot, etc.) in your script. That will be up to the director to decide. You also don't need to include transition directions from one scene to the next.

Here's an example:

EXT. GEORGE WASHINGTON HIGH SCHOOL – DAY

Students mill around in front of school. A bell RINGS. Students stream into the building.

INT. A CLASSROOM – DAY

STUDENTS enter the classroom. JENNIFER, 16, and TANISHA, 16, sit at desks next to each other and begin whispering and pointing to KYLE, 17, who is sporting a black eye.

JENNIFER

What happened to you, Kyle? Did your little sister beat you up again?

Tanisha laughs while Kyle silently fumes.

Research/Writing Assignment:

Watch a movie that you've seen often enough so that you already know the plot. Take notes while you watch. What images are used to tell the story? How is character conveyed through action and dialogue? Notice where there is tension. How is the tension expressed? Write a paper detailing the significant aspects of the movie.

Or you may choose to write a short screenplay of five to ten pages. You might try adapting your short play to a screenplay format.

Unit Three

Story

Chapter Thirteen
Tell Me a Story!

You've already learned a lot about story by examining character development and plot in the unit on scene. In Part Three, we'll look at how those concepts apply to narrative prose, and we'll also explore those aspects of writing that are specific to narrative prose.

Types of Narrative Prose

In this section you'll practice writing imaginative prose. You may be writing creative nonfiction or fiction. Fiction comes in several formats:

- short, short stories or flash fiction (usually under 500 words)
- short stories (anywhere between 500 and 20,000 words)
- novellas (from 20,000 to 50,000 words)
- novels (more than 50,000 words)

Creative nonfiction can be divided similarly:

- personal essays (250-1500 words)
- narrative essays (1,500 to 35,000 words)
- book-length memoir or journalism (more than 35,000 words)

To complicate matters, there is also a category called the "prose poem," a hybrid form of poetry written in a paragraph style rather than with line breaks. There's even a journal online dedicated to the prose poem called "The Prose Poem," which can be found at www.webdelsol.com. The prose poem and the short-short story or flash fiction are similar and the labels may be interchangeable in some cases.

Prose Style

Style is how you bring your internal qualities to the surface and allow people to understand something about your character, ideals, and cultural context. People may dress in ways that show a certain style. We have styles of speaking, walking, dancing, and so forth, which express both our individuality and our affiliation with or affinity to social and cultural groups.

When we speak of good writing style, we generally mean writing that grabs our attention and then keeps our attention. We usually like writing that flows well and has a musical quality. But sometimes a writer may use a choppy style. It all depends on the effect he wants to create. The style of prose will communicate something not only about the quality of the story, but also about its relationship with the world outside the story. Your writing style is determined by the following:

- Diction: do you use multisyllabic, difficult words or short, simple words? Do you tend to use slang or write in a formal tone?
- Verbs: do you use strong, active verbs or passive verbs?
- Sentence construction: do you have lots of short, choppy sentences strung together or long, complicated sentences or something in between?
- Structure: is the piece of writing straightforward and to the point or do you make digressions, investigating topics as they occur to you?
- Pacing: do you plunge from one topic or scene to the next? Or is your writing more placid and slow-moving?

Individual writers may vary their style, depending on the topic and depending on the effect they want to create. But sometimes certain writers come to be identified with a certain style. For example, Ernest Hemingway was credited with popularizing "minimalism," a writing style that appears very simple. Sentences are short. Descriptions are spare. Words are generally easy to understand. William Faulkner, on the other hand, had a more loquacious style. His sentences can ramble on for great stretches, and you may need to look up the meanings of some of his words.

This is the opening of Hemingway's story, "The Killers." Notice how succinct Hemingway is.

"The door of Henry's lunchroom opened and two men came in. They sat down at the counter."

You can see there's not much description and the diction is simple and straightforward. William Faulkner's style, on the other hand, is very different. Here is the second sentence of the opening paragraph of his short story, "Barn Burning:"

"The boy, crouched on his nail keg at the back of the crowded room, knew he smelled cheese, and more: from where he sat he could see the ranked shelves close-packed with the solid, squat, dynamic shapes of tin cans whose labels his stomach read, not from the lettering which meant nothing to his mind but from the scarlet devils and the silver curve of fish - this, the cheese which he knew he smelled and the hermetic meat which his intestines believed he smelled coming in intermittent gusts momentary and brief between the other constant one, the smell and sense just a little of fear because mostly of despair and grief, the old fierce pull of blood."

Writers develop their writing styles over the course of many years. Your style may not be evident in your first piece of writing, and you may want to experiment with different styles until you find the one that is just right for you. Even then, you will probably modify your style as your vocabulary changes, your life experiences start piling up, and your goals as a writer mature.

What Do You Know?

Earlier in the book we discussed that old adage: "write what you know." Even though you may be writing fiction, this can still be good advice. For some writers, this presents no problem. They already find their lives endlessly fascinating and have been observing the daily events that occur in their lives with great curiosity, possibly even writing copious journals on the ins and outs of their day-to-day adventures.

But for other beginning writers, this may present a problem. They may think that they don't know much of anything and that the things they do know are boring. Here's a piece of advice: don't worry if the events you write about are boring or not—an obviously exciting event won't necessarily make a more compelling story than an ostensibly boring one. The art is in the telling, and while you may think your life is mundane, someone who does not have your experiences or your background may find your perspective fascinating.

When writers write what they know, they write with authority. Their descriptions will be true, the dialogue authentic, and the events they describe will be original and not poor imitations of someone else.

The Narrative Essay

Most of the essays you write in school are to demonstrate your knowledge of a particular subject or your ability to expound on a subject chosen by someone else. The narrative essay is easier in some ways because if there's one topic on which you are an expert, it is yourself, but it's also difficult to do justice to your own experiences or to structure those experiences in a meaningful way.

The narrative essay tells the story of a true event in your life and shows how that event has affected the present or even the future. Or it may be based on a particular aspect of your life that draws on several different events or time periods as in the case of Annie Dillard's essays. An essay is not merely the recitation of an anecdote, however. The narrative essay also reflects on the significance of the events.

To write a narrative essay, do the following:

- Write down a list of five to ten things that have happened in your life.
- Choose one that seems meaningful to you.
- Write down what happened.
- Include some commentary about what the event or events mean to you.

Topics might include:

- winning or losing some kind of game
- learning a lesson when you did something wrong
- a lesson you learned from a sibling, friend, parent, or teacher
- any "first" – first kiss, first date, first crush, first time driving a car, first day at school or at ballet class or football practice
- a trip somewhere
- holidays with your family
- a bad day at work or school
- peculiar quirks in your family

Putting the Creative in Creative Nonfiction

Narrative or personal essays are considered creative nonfiction. But what makes them "creative"?

- First of all, a narrative essay tells a story or a series of stories with a point. This entails selection. If you're telling a story from your life, there may be a lot of things you leave out. If you included every single detail, a single story might be a hundred pages long. So it is up to the writer to select those aspects of the story that are most interesting and that are most meaningful.
- Secondly, the events can be arranged so they form something resembling a plot. You can include tension, conflict, plot twists, a climax and a resolution.
- Third, description, dialogue and action, all the elements of a scene, enliven a narrative of any kind. Scenes are the lifeblood of narrative because they help the reader to see, hear and experience the story as if he or she were there.
- Finally, in essay writing you can use the same figurative language and poetic devices that you use in poetry: similes, metaphor, personification, alliteration, irony and so on.

In many ways, the narrative or personal essay is similar to the short story. In creative nonfiction, however, the writer is more likely to provide some commentary on the story while in fiction the writer generally lets the story speak for itself; however, this is not a hard and fast rule.

Turning Essays into Entertainment

Annie Dillard is probably the most well-known creative nonfiction writer living in America today. Her topics include childhood, writing, and American culture. She is admired for her thoughtful, intelligent writing as well as her lyrical descriptions. Her books include *Pilgrim at Tinker Creek* and *An American Childhood*.

David Sedaris is another writer who has turned his life into wonderful, and sometimes hilarious, personal narratives. Sedaris began by telling stories on NPR. Now he has several books and regularly goes on tour to tell his stories to packed auditoriums.

The Moth Radio Hour is an outlet for people to tell their true stories. It airs on more than 200 stations around the country. You can see videos of their stories on themoth.org.

Research Assignment:

Read this essay by Annie Dillard: "Christmas Books: The Leg In The Christmas Stocking: What We Learned From Jokes."

Published in The New York Times. (http://partners.nytimes.com/books/99/03/28/specials/dillard-christmas.html) Make a list of creative writing techniques (description, character, plot) that you noticed and examples and bring it to class for discussion.

Blog Assignment:

Choose two different prose writers and read passages from their work, comparing the different styles. Suggested writers include Toni Morrison, James Baldwin, David Sedaris, James Joyce, Flannery O'Connor, Eudora Welty, Raymond Carver, Shirley Jackson, Chuck Palahniuk, George R.R. Martin, Suzanne Collins, or any writer you especially admire. Now write a paragraph imitating the style of one of the writer you chose but with a different topic.

Vocabulary

Define the following and add any new words that you have encountered recently:

Adage

Anecdote

Articulate (adjective)

Hermetic

Loquacious

Ostensibly

Syntax

Writing Prompts

1. Do a free write beginning with the words: "I remember…"

2. Blueprint

    - Draw a blueprint or map of the house or apartment where you lived when you were between the ages of six and eight.
    - Where are the bedrooms, the living room, etc.?
    - Draw the yard or street outside.
    - Now think back. What events occurred during this time period? Put "x" marks at the places where anything important happened.
    - Now choose the most important event and free write about it. Describe everything you can remember. Who else was with you? What did you feel and think at the time?

Chapter Fourteen
Making It Up

A fictional short story is a particular type of art. It is generally told from one character's point of view (sometimes in the first person and sometimes in the third person). It can be told in the present tense or in the past tense. It is usually an exploration of a small period of time in a person's life.

Here are some guidelines for writing an effective short story.

To write an effective short story you should:

- Start quickly. Short stories must get to the heart of the matter in the first paragraph.
- Limit the scope of the story to one main problem. Short story writing requires focusing in on one main issue and exploring it fully.
- Limit the number of characters and scenes. You don't have much room in a short story to introduce and develop characters, so stick with two or three.
- Include only those details essential to understanding the story. Long-winded descriptions of places or objects that have no bearing on the story usually just distract the reader.
- Limit your short story to a short time period. You can't adequately cover your character's entire life or even a few years in a short story.

Mining for Material

Some short stories may take place in a purely fictional world, but most contemporary short story writers set their stories in a reality that bears a strong resemblance to real life. And many writers use the world that they know best as the basis for their stories.

So how does a writer turn events from his life or someone else's life into fiction? This is both the easiest and the hardest task facing a writer.

Here are three guidelines that will help:

1. Don't be shackled by the truth. Just because something really happened that way, doesn't mean that it is believable, interesting or meaningful. It is your job to make it so.
2. Be selective. Choose those events, incidents, images, etc. that contribute to the meaning of the story.
3. Allow visual images and sensory details to convey the heart of the story.

Steps for turning a factual story into a fictional story:

- Change the basic character elements of the real person: name, appearance, background, sometimes even gender.
- Intensify the conflict; bring out the unsaid and the undone.
- Give your character insights that he or she might not have had at the time.
- If the story is about you, try writing at least a draft in the third person.
- Find those images or objects (either natural or human-made) that give symbolic weight to the story and use them.
- Eliminate any scene, dialogue, etc. that doesn't contribute to the meaning.

Research

Many writers research subjects that interest them in order to get good stories. You can interview other people, such as your parents, your grandparents, or a friend who is from another country or another cultural background. Find out what their lives were like before you knew them. You might ask your grandparents how they met or ask your mother or father about their school days. You can also talk to professionals, such as fire fighters, police officers, lawyers, or doctors. Visit a retirement facility. The elderly usually love to talk about their lives. The more you know about people and their lives, the more depth your writing will have.

Your academic classes can also provide material. Writers often incorporate facts and ideas from philosophy, history, science, or other fields into their writing.

Go places and do things. When you go somewhere, learn about the history of the place. Notice the buildings and the landscape. Describe those places in your journal. Do things you haven't done before. Sign up for skydiving lessons or ballroom dancing. Everything you do can become material.

Read, of course. Read biographies, history, whatever you can find about the topic that interests you.

Charlotte Perkins Gilman -- A Revolutionary

Charlotte Perkins Gilman lived from 1860 to 1935, a time when women had few political or social rights. Middle and upper class women were not expected to work or to engage in intellectual activities. Their role was to be in the home, and their duty was to be happy and cheerful. If a woman chose an independent life as a writer, for instance, others often ridiculed her. Women were often thought to be victims of "hysteria."

After the birth of her only child, Gilman experienced post-partum depression but the treatment was worse than the disease. It was also the inspiration for her most famous short story, "The Yellow Wallpaper."

Research Assignment:

Read "The Yellow Wallpaper." It can easily be found online or in most libraries.

Then write a brief response for discussion.

Blog Assignment:

Make a list of 10 to 15 "strong" verbs -- verbs that convey action and have emotional impact.

Student Writing Sample

In this sample, D'Avva uses poetic language, strong verbs, and complex sentences to create an atmosphere of foreboding.

A tempest raged outside, thrashing and slashing at anything that stood in her path. Her scream of anger echoed in the hills, the shrill whistle sending shivers down even the toughest of spines. The window panes shuddered in their frames and the house groaned from the onslaught. I was so thankful papa had caulked the walls the day before or we would be dealing with weather inside and out. The trees danced a violent samba just beyond our window, the leaves snatched from their cradles and thrown into the air to be lost into the deluge. Mama sat in her rocking chair, her unfinished quilt draped over her lap as she sewed on another patch. Her swollen belly barely allowed the quilt to cover her. Papa was pacing before the door, the veins in his neck and face wiggling beneath his skin. He was worried for Mama and our sibling. My own heart was racing faster than our wolf-dog, Shadow. I reached down and sank my fingers into the warm pelt of the dog. His body uttered a soft sigh as I gave him gentle comfort. Lightning violently smacked the earth only feet from our window and my pulse leapt into my throat. Shadow uttered the softest of growls, but Mama shushed him. "We've needed the rain. Let us be thankful for it." I looked at Mama, her voice calm and without worry, but her brow was knit. Our sibling was due soon.

-- D'Avva Holiday

Vocabulary

Identify and define at least five words from your readings:

Writing Prompt

Think back to an important event in your past. Really spend some time in this experience. What are the sensory details that you can bring to mind? What did this experience mean to you? Think of an object or image that might convey that meaning. Questions: Where are you? What do you see, above, below, all four sides? What do you hear? Are there any smells? Who is with you? What are you wearing, holding, thinking? Insert two sentences of dialogue.

Write about that event and add an element that didn't happen: something that will cause the meaning to come into sharper relief. For example, let's say the event you chose is a time you were hanging out with some friends. You remember there was a lot of tension but no one said anything. In your fictional account, have the characters bring up the problem. Maybe in real life, the problem was resolved, but in your story the problem expands and gets worse.

Chapter Fifteen
Character Development in the Prose Narrative

In her book *Writing Fiction*, Janet Burroway writes: "your fiction can only be as successful as the characters who move it and move within it. Whether they are drawn from life or are pure fantasy—and all fictional characters lie somewhere between the two—we must find them interesting, we must find them believable and we must care about what happens to them."

There are some fictional characters you just can't forget: Captain Ahab, Huck Finn, Hannibal Lector, Janie Mae Crawford, Scout Finch, Bigger Thomas, and the Cat in the Hat to name a few. These characters are memorable because the writer managed to make us care about them even if they cause destruction.

Readers need to know who the main character of the story is early in the process of reading. Something should connect them to that character. That doesn't mean that your main character needs to be flawless. In fact, we tend to relate to characters that have a few flaws. Even if your main character isn't likable, he or she should be interesting.

Characters are not real people. They are in your story to serve a purpose, and so they usually aren't as complex as someone you actually know. That doesn't mean that characters have to be predictable, but they must behave in ways that your readers believe they could behave.

There are generally three types of characters in fiction:

- Major characters, or protagonists (heroes both male and female) and antagonists (villains)
- Supporting Roles: partners, friends, family members and people who help or hinder the heroes or villains
- Minor characters: bystanders (In a short story you will generally not have a lot of minor characters.)

Revealing Character

In the prose narrative, there are four typical methods for revealing character:

- physical description – what does he or she look like?
- action – what does he or she do?
- voice or dialogue – what does he or she say?
- interior monologue – what does he or she think?

Physical Description

Often a driver's license description is not the most effective way to describe the appearance of your character. Instead of telling us that is a character is 6 feet 5 inches tall, why not say he had to stoop over when coming through the doorway or mention that he towered over others. The best descriptions generally tell us something about the character's personality.

Here's a description from a short story by Anton Chekhov that tells us a good deal about a man and his wife: "He was under forty, but he had a daughter already twelve years old, and two sons at school. He had been married young, when he was a student in his second year, and by now his wife seemed half as old again as he. She was a tall, erect woman with dark eyebrows, staid and dignified, and, as she said of herself, intellectual...and he secretly considered her unintelligent, narrow, inelegant, was afraid of her, and did not like to be at home."

We tend to remember characters' distinguishing features. Everyone knows the color of Ron Weasley's hair as well as where Harry Potter's scar is and what it looks like. Provide your reader with enough information to form a mental picture of the character. Then let the action, dialogue and thoughts do the rest.

Rita Mae Brown in her book *Starting from Scratch* says: "Characters are almost always composites plus a touch of imagination." So borrow a nervous habit from one person, a certain mode of speech from someone else, and perhaps a style of dress from a third. Add these "real people" qualities to your fictional characters to flesh them out.

Action

Active characters are more interesting than passive characters. Show your character doing something, such as working or playing. We should also be able to "see" what happens during periods of dialogue. What do they do while they are conversing? Do they walk around the room? Do they pick up objects and play with them? Do they have any nervous habits? Get your characters out and about. Make them mingle and mix with others. See what happens.

The most important thing you can give your main character is a goal. A character that wants something and is willing to go after it pulls the reader into her predicament.

Voice

Voice is that quality of writing that sets either the narrator or the characters apart. Voice will establish your character's uniqueness and make her interesting to the reader. The voice should sound individual and reflect the personality traits of the character.

Character voice can reflect any number of aspects of character including:

- Place of origin
- Socio-economic status (or class)

- Ethnicity
- Age
- Educational level
- Gender
- Emotional state

Here's an example from the short story "The Lesson" by Toni Cade Bambara:

> *Back in the days when everyone was old and stupid or young and foolish and me and Sugar were the only ones just right, this lady moved on our block with nappy hair and proper speech and no makeup. And quite naturally we laughed at her, laughed the way we did at the junk man who went about his business like he was some big-time president and his sorry-ass horse his secretary.*

What can you tell about this character just from the voice?

A strong voice gives your character authority and authenticity. Readers must feel they are in sure hands. They must believe the character is really the type of person you are trying to portray.

Some people have a certain idiolect -- words they use frequently, or syntactic constructions that are normal in their speech patterns. These modes of communication are what give us (and our characters) individuality. Some writers even invent their own language.

The following example of an idiolect shows just how original you can be when creating character voice. This is from a short story by Ron Wiginton, published in *Black Warrior Review*, called "The Blood Rushing Face Thing."

> *Jason Bason and I ride south to 47th, catch a pass to Broad Street and then walk two blocks to the Automatic School. That's where The O'Dougal Man teaches. Yesterday he and Danny Franny were dip dancing in the hallway and that's why Danny Franny is now maintaining juvenile time with the county. And that's why Jason Bason and I and most C-Boys make sure we get to school on time. Today The O'Dougal Man gets warm.*

Dialogue in Narrative Prose

Dialogue is key to character development and understanding. As in drama, dialogue should be believable but doesn't necessarily need to be realistic. In other words, when we speak to each other every day, we say a lot of stuff that just isn't very interesting. A lot of the "Hi, how are you" chitchat that goes on in every day conversation isn't necessary in fiction. In dialogue, you cut right to the chase.

Dialogue can be used to do the following:

- Establish and develop character
- Convey information
- Create tension
- Relay subtext

To become good at dialogue, do the following:

- listen to people speak
- jot down unusual speech constructions
- make sure the dialogue you write serves more than one purpose

Please use tag lines. Some beginning writers think that it becomes monotonous to use "he said" and "she said." Actually, the reader barely notices those tags. You can vary them by using words such as asked, responded, and so on, but there's no need to overdo it. Occasionally you can get away with dropping the tag, but remember it can be extremely frustrating for a reader not to be able to identify who is speaking.

Interior Monologue

This is one of the most useful devices for establishing and developing character. Interior monologue means telling us what the character is saying to herself or himself. The interior monologue lets us know what the character is thinking and feeling.

Example:

> *Nothing had been touched in the empty room. I was alone and the room where I had once been so happy now seemed like a dungeon. Where was my wife? What would I do now? I felt my pockets. I had no money, no friends, no family. I began to think of places where I could go to hide, but nothing seemed right. I heard someone moan and realized the sound had come from my own throat. What was I to do?*

Interior monologue is a device that can be used frequently. We like to know what a character is thinking and feeling. It helps the reader to get emotionally involved in the story.

Now, of course, you don't want to have interior monologues from all your characters unless you're writing an experimental piece. In fact, most writers choose a single point of view character, and the events of the story are filtered through that character's thoughts. Dipping into the minds of more than one character in a short piece will cause your reader to wonder whom they should care about.

Character Change

In fiction the main character is usually (but not always) changed by the events of the story. The character may have an epiphany, in which he or she discovers something about life or about himself or herself. If a character gets maimed or killed, that's obviously a change, but that's not the type of change that makes a great short story. The type of change we mean is an interior change – a way of thinking or feeling.

Blog Assignment:

Describe your bedroom or some other room where you spend a lot of time. Be specific. If there are posters or pictures on the wall, who is in them? If there are books on the shelf, what are some of the titles? What kinds of furnishings are in the room? Help us to see the room, and let the details of the room tell the reader about you.

Student Writing Sample

Sometimes we can show character or plot through environment. Here is a description of a character's environment that helps to develop a plot as well.

The kitchen was in a shambles. The normally neat counter was littered with the shriveled crumbs of chopped vegetables that had dehydrated with time. A mountain of dishes balanced in the sink, teetering on the brink of an avalanche from the slightest touch. Last week's dinner was carelessly tossed to the side and still sat decomposing and growing that fuzzy green mold. It was obvious that something wasn't quite right. Fred was typically a clean person. Acquaintances might even classify him as a neat freak. He was obsessive almost to the point of OCD, especially about his kitchen.

In fact, upon a second glance, you could tell that the kitchen should have been pristine, and that in its traditional state, it would take on an appearance of grandeur. Marble counter tops stretched out from wall to wall. There was enough room to cook for a small village even though Fred was a bachelor. Above the counters, ornate wooden cupboards reflected a peaceful, warming glow from crystal chandeliers. If you were to open the cupboards, you would find that every single thing was labeled -- from the shelf for pots and pans down to the segmented and compartmentalized drawer of fresh herbs, where masking tape detailed the contents of each as well as the date that it was placed there.

Clearly something was not right.

-- Jeffrey Harris

Vocabulary

Define the following and add any new words that you have encountered recently:

Composite

Epiphany

Idiolect

Syntax

Tag lines

Writing Prompts

1.   Write a scene showing someone at work. What happens when something goes wrong?

2. Show us a character through physical description, dialogue, action, and interior monologue.

Chapter Sixteen
Scene and Summary

In fiction writing, the writer employs two devices: telling (summary) and showing (scene). One common mistake that beginning fiction writers make is that they often tell rather than show, relying more on summary than scene. Both of these techniques are important but sometimes the writer will simply summarize events that would be more effective if they were fleshed out in a scene. See the examples below:

> **Summary:** I walked with my friend Caitlin to school so she wouldn't get hurt by the bully girls again.

> **Scene:** I knocked on door of Caitlin's house. She opened it up and looked at me in surprise.
>
> "I wanted to make sure you made it to school today," I said.
>
> Caitlin grabbed her books from a table by the door and came outside.
>
> "Thanks," she mumbled. Her long brown hair was dirty, and her eyes looked tired. I wondered what her home life was like.
>
> As we got near the school, Karen and Shaunice were waiting on the corner. Karen nudged Shaunice when she saw us. Caitlin tensed up.
>
> "Keep walking," I said. "They won't hurt you."
>
> We walked past them. Karen and Shaunice glared at us, but they didn't do anything. They didn't dare.

The scene has dialogue, action, description and even interior monologue. Now, sometimes the event you're describing doesn't need all that. In that case, then you write a summary as in the first example, but for important events, a scene helps the readers experience it for themselves.

Here's a game called *Tell and Show*. The first line is telling something. Then you write down an example that shows it:

Example:

Tell: He loves her.

Show: He gives her roses every day.

Tell: She is a nice person.

Show:

Tell: I had a horrible day.

Show:

Tell: That guy is a real jerk.

Show:

Tell: He lives in a nice house.

Show:

Tell: We were so scared.

Show:

Writing Effective Scenes

As in drama, scene in narrative prose allows you to do the following:

- develop character
- move the action forward
- fill in background information

But there's more to it, of course, than merely writing down what happens. Whenever possible you want to craft the scene. That is, you want to create a sense of "thereness" for your readers and you do this by paying careful attention to sensory details. You've practiced writing dialogue and action in your dramatic piece. In prose you have two more tools: description and interior monologue.

Here are some questions to ask yourself when crafting a scene:

- What season of the year are we in?
- What is the weather like?
- Is your character cold or hot or somewhere in between?
- What is the light like?
- What time of day is it?
- What is the light source?
- Are your characters indoors or out?
- If inside, what room are they in?
- How big is the room?
- What furnishings are in the room?
- What sounds besides dialogue are the characters hearing?
- What do they smell?
- What do they see?
- Bring in some dialogue to reveal character and/or push the plot forward. Change what they are saying.
- What do the characters do as they talk?
- What does your main character think when she is not talking?

Of course, not every scene brings in every one of these aspects. Some scenes are shorter and less involved, but knowing how to develop and craft a fully rendered scene will not only help you to convey more information to your reader, it will also bring a deep sense of pleasure to your reader.

Layering a Scene

You can write a scene with just dialogue or just action or even just internal monologue. But for some scenes, you'll want to incorporate all of the possibilities.

Here's a step-by-step process for layering a scene:

Step One: Write a dialogue between two characters. Just dialogue.

Jorge: I wish you wouldn't just assume you think you know what I mean.

Alyssa: Well, I'm not a moron. I do understand basic vocabulary. It's not like you're speaking Greek.

Jorge: But you willfully misinterpret what I say.

Alyssa: Then maybe you could just be clearer.

Step Two: Add character action:

"I wish you wouldn't just assume you think you know what I mean," Jorge said, slamming the book on the table.

Alyssa set her coffee cup down.

"Well, I'm not a moron," she said. She pointed a finger at Jorge and continued, "I do understand basic vocabulary. It's not like you're speaking Greek."

Jorge sighed and glanced out the window.

"But you willfully misinterpret what I say."

"Then maybe you could be clearer," she replied and finished her cup of coffee.

Step Three: Add description.

Jorge walked into the cluttered coffee shop. His cheeks were red from the cold, and his hair stood on his head in a dark, disheveled mess. He looked as if he hadn't shaved in days.

"I wish you wouldn't just assume you think you know what I mean," Jorge said, slamming the book on the table. The customers at the next table watched curiously.

Alyssa set her coffee cup down on the worn wood and stood.

"Well, I'm not a moron," she said. She pointed a finger at Jorge and continued, "I do understand basic vocabulary. It's not like you're speaking Greek."

Jorge sighed and glanced out the window. The snow was falling like delicate lace.

"But you willfully misinterpret what I say." His voice was softer now.

"Then maybe you could be clearer," she replied and sat back down to finish her cup of coffee.

Step Four: Add interior monologue.

Jorge walked into the cluttered coffee shop. His cheeks were red from the cold, and his hair stood on his head in a dark, disheveled mess. He looked as if he hadn't shaved in days. Alyssa wondered what she had ever seen in him.

"I wish you wouldn't just assume you think you know what I mean," Jorge said, slamming the book on the table. The customers at the next table watched curiously.

Alyssa set her coffee cup down on the worn wood and rose. She had taken about as much crap from him as she could stand. He always thought he was so superior, so much smarter than she was.

"Well, I'm not a moron," she said. She pointed a finger at Jorge and continued, "I do understand basic vocabulary. It's not like you're speaking Greek."

Jorge sighed and glanced out the window. The snow was falling like delicate lace. Alyssa remembered the night before when the two of them had been wrapped in a warm blanket before the fire.

"But you willfully misinterpret what I say." His voice was softer now.

"Then maybe you could be clearer," she replied and sat back down to finish her cup of coffee. It was good coffee, rich and dark. She wouldn't let this argument ruin her enjoyment of it.

The Importance of Tension in a Scene

A scene needs to move the story forward. Something important should happen. Something should change. It should get worse or get better. Open conflict or buried tension is the driving force in a scene. It makes the scene go forward. So even if there's just a small amount of tension, tease it out, find it and bring it to the surface through any of the four elements described above: dialogue, action, description or interior monologue.

How to Write Dialogue in Prose Narrative

Did you notice in the example above that each time a new character speaks, the writer creates a new paragraph? It makes it much easier to read dialogue when a new paragraph indicates every time a different character speaks. Secondly, look at the punctuation. The comma or period goes inside the quotation mark.

Tag lines, as mentioned before, also help the reader. You may get bored with them but you don't want your reader to wonder who is speaking. Unless it is very clear who is speaking, use a tag line. Generally, for tag lines we write: "Jerome said" instead of "said Jerome" unless you have some sort of description of Jerome that comes right after the tag, such as in the following example:

"Excuse me," said Jerome, who was blowing his nose profusely.

When do you use a comma and when do you use a period? Use a comma before a tag.

Example: "I don't know," Jerome said.

Use a period if there is no tag after the dialogue.

Example: "I don't know," Jerome said. "I will have to ask my brother."

When one character addresses another, use a comma to indicate this is a form of direct address. There is a world of difference between: "Let's eat Raoul" and "Let's eat, Raoul."

Scene and Setting

In an interview, writer Bob Shacochis once said that if writing didn't have a strong sense of place then it was most likely "McFiction." In other words writing that doesn't have a strong setting has no character. Your setting may be your backyard or it might be in Tasmania, but wherever it is, render it clearly and accurately. Give us a sense of the place and how it affects the characters. Everyone is affected by place.

Here's an example of good setting. It's a passage from *Amy and Isabelle* by Elizabeth Strout:

> *Mill Road was what Main Street became once it crossed over the bridge and*
> *while Mill Road did lead eventually to the mill, it first wound itself through a section*
> *of stores that included an old A & P with sawdust on its floors, a furniture outlet*
> *with faded couches in the windows, a few clothing stores and coffee shops, a*
> *pharmacy that for years had had the same display of a dusty plastic African violet*
> *sitting in the middle of a bedpan.*

There are just enough details to give us a sense of a rundown but still functioning town. We don't need to know the name of the pharmacy but that little detail of the dusty African violet helps us know exactly what kind of drugstore it is.

Interior settings are equally important and can tell us much about the characters who inhabit them. Anne Lamott, in her book by *Bird by Bird*, says: "Every room gives us layers of information about our past and present and who we are, our shrines and quirks and hopes and sorrows, our attempts to prove that we exist . . ."

Sharpen Your Powers of Description

Writers often wonder what to describe and what not to describe? How to describe? Why describe? Generally, in contemporary narrative, you want to give enough description for your reader to feel "grounded."

Description does the following:

- Helps us see the characters
- Helps create a mood
- Helps us see the setting
- Gives us a sense of where the characters are
- Lets us know what the characters are doing

Some writers are very straightforward in their descriptions. Others use a more lyrical style that creates a mood as well as showing what there is to see.

Here's a description of Hawaii from Pamela Ball's novel, *Lava*:

> *On the Big Island there are places which are marked for death, where the land itself waits like a hungry mouth. The sharp curve of highway up on Polipoli Pass that caught hold of teenagers driving late at night, the constant threat of the volcano erupting, the riptide at the edge of the bay, the rows of poisonous oleander trees planted too near a barbecue pit in the public parks, where sometimes a visitor broke off a branch to roast a hot dog and was dead before the second bite.*

On the other hand, lengthy descriptions may bog down your narrative. In the 19th century you could get away with writing a six-page description before ever getting into the action, but Ernest Hemingway changed the way most contemporary English-language writers approach description. Even the most ardent stylist keeps descriptions in check. We want to see where we are, for instance, in a subway station with advertisements for toothpaste on the walls and a sleeping drunk lying on the floor. But then we're ready for action.

Use meaningful descriptions

We don't need to know the color of the couch where your character is sitting unless color is important thematically or unless there is something unusual about the color. But if you are the sort of person who knows a Duncan Phyfe table from an IKEA dinette set, then feel free to put those details in—especially when they reveal character. Do research, whenever necessary, to give an accurate and authentic picture. But always remember your descriptions are there to serve the story, not vice versa.

Just as in poetry, sensory details such as the sights, sounds, tastes, smells and the touch of things in your story will help your readers feel more connected to it.

The time of the season

While place and description are important to the setting, so is the time period. If you're writing a story about racism, it will be a very different story if it's set in 1950 than if it's set in 2005. You don't have to come right out and say what year the story is set although some writers do. You can let readers know by the clothes your characters wear, how they speak, the music that is playing, and the things that are going on at the time. If a character says something is "swell," your reader will assume that this is a story set in the past.

Seasonal cues and the weather add atmosphere to a story and help your reader feel as if she is right there with the characters. Does one of your characters shiver in a thin sweater, or is he sweltering under the summer sun?

When to Use Summary

If an entire narrative prose piece is written in scenes, it will take a very long time to write. Generally, in narrative prose there is a balance. The important events are rendered in scenes, but summary helps transition between scenes, indicate the passage of time, provide background information, and provide reflection.

Journalism makes great use of summary and will generally include only brief scenes. Some narrative essays tend more toward the journalistic summary end of the spectrum.

Research Assignment:

Re-read your favorite short story or essay and count the number of scenes. What is the purpose of the scenes? Is there a balance between scene and summary? If not, which is more? Why?

Writing Assignment:

Begin developing the characters and creating a strong setting for your narrative prose piece. It can be creative nonfiction or it can be fiction. You may use the prompts at the end of this chapter to help you get started.

Student Writing Samples

Here's a response to a scene writing exercise from student writer Kelsey Armour. Notice the clues that let the reader know the time period.

Unfamiliar Conversation

Jessi twirls her fork around in her massive heap of noodles and lifts it to her mouth, sucking in long strings of tomatoey noodles and coating her lips with parmesan and sauce.

"Jess," her dad says, sipping on a Stella and giving her the eye. She rolls her eyes.

Kim, Jessi's mom, gets up for another glass of wine and remarks that the color of the room makes her skin look washed out and it needs to be changed as soon as possible. She says she would prefer something like periwinkle which would perfectly compliment her complexion. Russell eats with his hands, dipping his bread into the pasta and making sure to swipe up every last bit of sauce. Jessi notices how grotesque he is, lazy and pudgy, his fingers fat and wide like sausages, drenched in sauce, and groping for every last speck of food he could possibly fit in his body.

Ian sits beside her, fair and soft, with delicate eyes and shaggy hair, so fragile in the stages of early puberty with a zit growing directly on the tip of his nose. Their father babbles mindlessly about nothing unfamiliar: overpriced gasoline, the Bush administration, and how gay marriage should not even be a discussion.

Suddenly from behind his shaggy hair, Ian squeaks, "Dad, I'm gay."

The room goes quiet except for the sound of half-chewed spaghetti falling from gaping mouths. They focus their eyes not on Ian but on the huge pulsing vein in their father's forehead, bulging between bloodshot eyes as if he were about to explode at any second. He breathes, halfway smiles, and asks Jessi to pass the butter.

Here's an example of a short piece where the heat is almost a character in itself.

Porch

From the steps of the porch, Eli watched the old corn farmer rock slowly in his chair, hand shielding his eyes from the blinding rays of the sun.

"It's mighty hot out today," Eli called out to the ancient man, who seemed either to ignore him or was unable to hear. Eli paused a moment, waiting for a response, and dried his sweaty unused hand on the seat of his pants. He wore a pocket-sized Bible wrapped around his neck, bound with thin rope. After waiting a moment longer, Eli yelled louder than before,

"It's mighty hot out today!" As if startled from sleep, the old man looked down at the steps, where Eli stood expectantly.

"That it is, m'boy," the farmer said, squinting with wrinkled eyes. "My wife heard on the radio that it's the hottest it's been all summer."

"Yep," Eli said, thumbing the cover of his bible absent-mindedly. "A real scorcher."

"Yep," the old man agreed and seemed ready to end the conversation.

Eli blurted out, "Sir, do you need Jesus in your life?"

The old man blinked, surprised at the change of subject and irritated.

"I don't need no Jesus, thank you very much." The farmer huffed, crossing his arms and looking away. "I'm doing fine by myself, without the help a' any Jesus."

By the dismissal in the old man's voice, Eli understood that it was time to go home. He turned around; the sun now baking his neck and back. He wished he had brought a hat.

Alex Murphy

Following is the beginning of a story by Gabrielle Porter. She does a great job of staying in one character's point of view and incorporating interior monologue. The entire piece is comprised of two scenes in one setting.

Happiness for the Harmed

There she sits, in the library, trying to finish her homework, playing games on Facebook and listening to music through YouTube, trying to ignore the people around her and keep away the thoughts that plague her. She occasionally glances out the window to watch the weather. It's been cloudy all day and she's forgotten her umbrella. Her thoughts start to drift as she thinks about her past, present, and possible future. She's given life her best, but they all say it's never enough. It's gotten to the point where even she says her best isn't enough and she doesn't see any point in trying anymore. The only reason she tries at all is that, according to her parents, she has to.

The thoughts race through her head, following the same pattern. Today she had gotten her test back from one of her classes, and was disappointed with her grade. She knew it was her fault and that she was going to get not a good grade. She couldn't do it anymore. Her parents wouldn't, won't, let her quit school. She has to finish. She has to make them happy. She can't do anything, even if she tries her hardest. She shouldn't be—. She cuts the thought off and turns to her music, games, and homework. She tries to clear her mind to focus on her homework better.

As she battles herself and tries to focus on her homework instead of her games, someone comes up and stands next to her. She notices him out of the corner of her eye and looks up at him. He studies her with a mix of confusion and interest. She pauses her music, takes out one of her earbuds and waits for him to speak.

"Do you know how to work this printer?" he asks, waving his hand toward the printer behind her and then looks over toward the reference desk, where there are three other students waiting for the librarian to help them. "The librarian looks busy."

"Uh, yeah," she responds. "All you have to do swipe your id card and select your document. It's not that hard once you get used to it. Are you new here?"

"Yeah, I'm a freshman. My parents wanted me to learn something worthwhile, like business. I wanted to do film. Anyway, the printer back at our house decided to stop working."

"That must be annoying. Oh, and you should definitely go for whatever you want to do with film. This can be a back-up plan," she says, smiling a little. Then she sighs. "I have homework to do."

"You look familiar for some reason," he says.

She studies him and tries to figure out if she's seen him before.

"I think I've seen you before," she answers. "But I really don't know where. Must have seen you around campus these past few weeks." She turns back to the computer, not wanting to be bothered, since she knows the thoughts will come back if her music isn't playing, and she has homework that she waited until the last minute to do.

"Well, my name is Marcus, if you were wondering," he says.

She ignores him and puts her earbud back in, and goes to play her music again. He turns to leave while she sighs lightly and watches him leave out of the corner of her eye.

Marcus. The name sounds so familiar. She remembers her family's first house and one of her younger sister's birthday parties. They were having a three-legged race, and her mother said her sister won, while she knew that she and her partner had won. She believes her partner was named Marcus, while her sister was with Carson, Marcus's younger sister. She dismisses it as a coincidence; her friend lived in an entirely different state, or at least that was what her parents, and Facebook, told her. She thought it was New York or somewhere around there. She turns back to her homework, finds she cannot focus and turns to her games instead. She is lost in thought and tries her hardest to focus on her homework instead of her games.

Two hours pass as she alternates between her homework, choosing the next song she listens to, and playing her Facebook games. Then she senses the same someone who visited her two hours before. She looks up at him, takes an earbud out and is about to open her mouth to tell him to leave her alone. She hasn't gotten what she wanted to get done when she came into the library.

"I do know you," he says before she can get a sound out. "You're Amelia Smith, aren't you?"

She nods in response to his question.

"Don't you remember me? We were friends, what was it... eleven years ago?"

She nods again, shocked that a friend from her past, a friend she hasn't talked to in years, has somehow found her again.

"Yeah," she responds. "Marcus Jones." She smiles a little. "It's been eleven years and a couple of months. I was really upset that we had to move to Indiana." He laughs a little and sits at the empty computer on her other side. She swings in her chair to face him, not so angry anymore. Maybe the thoughts will stay away as she talks to him. She notices the song she was listening to has stopped, but she doesn't move to replay it.

"Do you still go by Ami?" he asks as he puts the backpack she didn't notice down. "With the weird spelling?"

"It isn't a weird way to spell it," she says, a little offended. "A-M-I is a perfectly acceptable way to spell Ami."

He smiles. "Sorry. A girl I knew in high school who spelled it A-M-Y and would get mad whenever I spelled it A-M-I."

"So I did spell it that way when I was younger," she says, her head tilting up a little as she tries to go to her past. His voice interrupts her attempts.

"You really don't remember much, do you?" he asks her, with a sad smile.

"No," she responds with a similar sad smile. "It's a bit of me not remembering things and a bit of being confused between memory and imagination."

"You always did have a good imagination. But exactly why do you have trouble remembering? That can't be the only reason."

She looks down at her lap as she answers. "Well, based on what I understand from my psychology class, it could be that I don't want to remember."

"Why?" he asks. He continues when she sits there looking at her lap. "You can tell me. I won't tell anyone else. And there's no one around."

She takes a deep breath. "I don't know exactly why, but I.... I couldn't take a joke. I felt like they laughed at me because of that." She sighs, but smiles, some positive thoughts coming up. "You know, I feel like I had a better life before we moved from Maryland. And you being here takes me back to when we were younger. Like when we 'spied' on your neighbors by jumping on the trampoline."

He laughs and says, "Yeah. Between us, Charlotte, and Carson, we came up with so many adventures."

She smiles, remembering some of those moments, like when they used the dryer vent at her family's house as a hand warmer in winter. She sees him smiling, too.

"It was your younger sister Charlotte who came up with the spelling of your nickname, wasn't it?" he asks her.

"Yeah," she says. "It was during the time we were playing at your house. We were jumping on the trampoline, like we usually were, weren't we?"

He smiles. "Yeah, I remember that. How is Charlotte, anyway?"

"She's good. She goes by Char now. Her friends came up with it. She'll graduate high school this year."

She frowns and looks down at her lap, trying to hold back the tears that were threatening to fall. "Of course, she's the smart one," she says, her voice catching a little.

"Hey, come on now," he says, like he knows exactly what she's feeling. "It's not that big of a deal. She has big plans for herself. What are your plans?"

She hesitates and then says, "Opening a place where people can go, no matter what they're like, or their past...."

He thinks about her answer and says, "That's why, isn't it? So you can have a place to go, to escape..."

"Yeah," she says quietly. "No one deserves to live a horrible life. But it happens anyway. They should have an actual place to escape that doesn't involve drugs or alcohol and where they can have a little fun. Be like a little kid without being judged."

"You can fulfill your dream and live the life you want no matter how smart or rich or dumb or poor you are. Just make sure you live." He smiles and stands up. He pauses before he picks up his backpack and kisses her forehead.

"I'll see you later," he says as he picks up his backpack and walks away. She sits there, shocked, while a small smile shows up on her slightly pink face.

Maybe there is hope for the future after all, she thinks.

Vocabulary

Define the following and add any new words that you have encountered recently:

Ardent

Pointillism

Trajectory

Writing Prompts

1. Imagine your character's kitchen or use your own. Now spend about five to ten minutes writing a descriptive passage of the kitchen that tells us something about the character.

2. Setting -- pick out a place that intrigues you. Now let two strangers encounter each other at that place. Write a short piece that incorporates setting into your scene.

Chapter Seventeen
What's Happening? Plot in Narrative Prose

You learned about plot when you wrote your play. As you work on your prose narrative, it's worth going over some of the fundamentals of plot as well as considering those elements of plot that apply specifically to prose narrative.

As you know, plot is the narrative sequence of cause and effect that gets your character(s) from the beginning to the end of the story. In a short story, the plot may be very simple. It's probably not going to have a lot of car chases or evil scientists threatening to destroy the world. The plot may be as simple as a young boy doing something wrong, or a woman moving out of the family home. Notice that a good plot begins with a person, a character, facing a situation.

Elements of Prose Plotting

Good plotting has been a concern of writers for centuries. Aristotle said the best plots work this way: "when the events come on us by surprise, and the effect is heightened when, at the same time, they follow as cause and effect. … The tragic wonder will then be greater than if they happened of themselves or by accident." According to Aristotle, pity and fear should spring out of the plot itself, and the plot should fit together as precisely as a puzzle. If an event or situation adds nothing to the story, then ditch it. For example, if there is an incidental car accident that interrupts the plot without altering its course, then you should eliminate that detail.

Things to consider when thinking about plot:

- Conflict and tension
- The stakes
- Plausibility
- Flashbacks
- Resolution and Theme

Conflict, tension, and stakes

Sometimes beginning writers are afraid to put their characters into scary or dangerous situations. They may see themselves or their friends in the characters and want to protect them. However if nothing happens (and this means bad things) then there won't be a story.

Look for the trouble or the problem in your character's situation. When you find it, start there! And when you start looking closer, you'll discover there's more trouble. Even when there is no outright conflict, there should be tension (the feeling that conflict is lurking somewhere underneath it all) in your scenes.

One thing that will make the story more compelling is if we know what is at stake. In other words, what does the main character stand to lose if he or she does not attain his or her goal? The stakes are the motivating force behind any narrative. The stakes are what feed the tension in the story and provide the momentum. Something has to matter to the main character. As you write your prose piece, ask yourself, what is at stake for your main character. Having something matter will drive the plot forward.

Flashbacks

The flashback is a useful device for letting us know a character's backstory, or what happened before the story began. Three things to avoid when using flashbacks

- flashbacks that are too long
- too many flashbacks
- flashbacks within flashbacks

A flashback can be as simple as a quick memory, which is relevant to the situation. Flashbacks as short as once sentence can help us better understand a situation.

Example:

For three weeks, John had purposely slammed me so hard it made my teeth rattle.

or

I remembered how John had grinned at me the first time I met him and how he told me he was going to beat me to a pulp the first chance he got.

Flashbacks help us understand the character's motives. Flashbacks can be longer than just a sentence—Proust's famous flashback covers hundreds of pages. They may be a paragraph or two in a short story or may be rendered in a full scene. However, if you spend too much time in flashback in a short piece, your reader will wonder what's the importance of the story's present time.

Plausibility

No matter how fantastic your story, most readers demand a qualified believability; you can have sentient alien squids and time travel, but your plot still has to move with intelligible cause and effect. The actions of your characters have to be explicable. Test your plot by asking "what if" and "why" questions:

- What if the character did something different?
- Why would the character do this?

One of the ways to establish plausibility is through the use of details. If you have created a world so real that the reader can see it, smell it, and feel the cold wind blowing, then your reader will be willing to suspend disbelief when you have a character that gets on a broom and flies.

Story Resolution and Theme

The resolution is the solution to the problem set up at the beginning of the story. Sometimes writers think they need a big blazing finale at the end, but in short fiction, the best ending may entail showing that the characters have changed somehow. Perhaps they have a greater understanding of their situation. Maybe your main character has resolved to change some aspect of his life. Perhaps her perspective has changed.

A short story may hinge on something small happening. For example: two teenage boys buy a gun. At the end of the story the boy who bought the gun throws it in a river. We realize he didn't care about owning it at all. He just needed the act of buying it. In a short story a character may learn something about herself or about someone she loves. We are not told the effect on the character. Instead we are shown the effect. Characters usually grow and change. They may become wiser, they may lose their innocence, or they may find the road to happiness.

Sometimes the writer will not end with a clear resolution. Some readers may find this frustrating, but a more sophisticated reader will realize it is up to them to decide how things will be. This is called an open resolution.

Gimmick endings such as "and then I woke up" have become clichés. It generally means the writer couldn't think of a way to get out of the situation they created.

To find a good ending for the story, you should ask yourself what is the point of the story? What is the underlying theme? Your ending should reflect that theme either through an image, dialogue, or a final thought. Sometimes you don't know what the theme of a story is until you get to the end. Then you realize exactly what it is you are trying to say.

Blog Assignment:

Make a list of things that have been important to you over your life. They can be tangible objects and they can also be the intangible things such as pride, self-esteem, etc.

Writing Assignment:

Continue to work on your piece of narrative prose, making sure that there is conflict and tension.

Student Writing Samples

Here's an example of a short-short story by student writer Alex Nunchuck about a boy who felt that the stakes in his life were pretty high.

The Menace

by Alex Nunchuk

I blame John almost as much as I blame myself. He broke the rules, he crossed the line, and I was sick of it. You see, John was on the other team, as always, and I'll admit we had our differences. He was rich, I was poor. He was aggressive, I thought I was passive.

The sacred huddle, that's where my team encircled to devise a battle plan.

John, though, he was a menace! So invading, so obtrusive! He continually snuck up to hear our plans, to cheat! And I had had enough.

The teams lined up on the gritty, sandy lot. I remember that at the last moment, the breeze had finally come, although to no relief. We were only dusted in the whirlwind of sand, enough to make my teeth crunch. I picked up a rock.

Time went fast, bodies started racing, the ball was moving, and John came for me. No thinking, only justice, my wrist snapped, and seconds after the play began, John was dazed, at his knees. Seeing the rock beside him, feeling the pounding of his skull, he began to whimper and wail.

No questions asked, no statements made, I went to the gym teacher. Feeling no guilt, only pride in accomplishing what I yearned for. I announced, "I took John down."

Following is a story about writing and about love.

Something New

by Rebecca Fisher

I didn't know her name. She was just the girl who had captured my attention more effectively and consistently than my psychology professor had ever succeeding in doing. Maybe if I knew her name she wouldn't seem so out of reach. As it was, the nameless girl was not only stunning, but she had a habit of correcting the instructor simply for her own amusement. I'll admit that I fell head over heels the first day when she said something that went way over my head but that I assumed was scientific and supremely intelligent because the professor nearly had a conniption trying to explain it to the rest of the class. I accidentally caught her gaze and the twinkling laughter in her eyes made the breath catch in my throat.

Those eyes saw everything, flicking around the room absorbing information so fast it must be the reason they were the same color of a stormy sea. Her lips, whether pulled back to release a full body laugh or sealed and tugged to the left corner to repress a caustic comment, never let a drop of that ocean pass, but I bet, if you kissed her it would taste like salt. Golden curls casually tangled around her face as if each morning the wind was her hairdresser but I couldn't imagine her any other way.

Sometimes, if I was lucky, she would look up when I was gawking and I could watch those dark lashes flutter demurely, teasing me in the same way her slightly chapped lips did when they curled up just the slightest bit. God, she was beautiful. She never dared to mark her skin with pigments or dyes and she didn't need them. With skin the color of sand lit by the moon and as flawless as porcelain it would be criminal to cover it.

My thoughts scattered like startled fish and I stiffened as a delicate finger tip traced the curve of my collar. Turning apprehensively, I glanced back to see the mercurial eyes that haunted my dreams. My breath caught in my throat.

"He's going over the topics for the final, you might want to listen," she murmured. She leaned so close I could smell the cinnamon gum she was chewing. Her breath tickled against my ear and I simply nodded trying not to let on the effect her voice had on me.

I could feel her smirk radiating from behind me and subtly smoothed the goose bumps that had made an appearance on my arms as I tried to pay attention to the professor's droning in the front of the lecture hall. The only thing I could focus on was the thought of how far she had had to lean forward in order to get that close. Soon movement fluttered throughout the students as they packed up books and laptops fleeing as quickly as they could hurtle over the students in front of them. A piece of paper appeared in front of me. Scribed in elegant looping cursive was the entirety of the exam expectations and across the top was the second most beautiful thing in the world: ten numbers, two parentheses, a dash and the name Morgan.

"I've kept a solid A in this class all term, so if you want a study buddy..." she left the question unsaid but understood.

I was jealous of her casual interaction with the world. She looked so at ease. Leaning against a lecture desk with a thumb hooked through a belt loop on a pair of jeans that hung just low enough that you could see a perfect stripe of pale flesh where her sheer blouse didn't quite cover. I pulled my gaze away, letting it drift up past the curve of her hips to a slender waist and higher still to the swell of her ribs that rounded out to a pleasant shape. It wasn't natural for someone's clavicle to be that enticing but the pendant that rested just above the swell of her breasts demanded my undivided attention. The brass bauble depicted a serpent curved into a crescent. My mind flickered back to the times I had noticed her idly hooking the tail over her lower lip or simply moving it back and forth over the well worn leather strand. Finally, I found her eyes, heat flushing my cheeks slightly as I wondered if she had noticed how long it took me to reply.

"That would be great; this class might be the death of me," I said hoping she would ignore the catch in my voice.

"My room, tomorrow, at eight?" she asked.

"Sounds good." I smiled, relieved when she grinned back.

I squinted into the sunshine as I left the classroom. Trapping my lip between my teeth to hide the stupid grin lurking in the creases of my face, I stuffed my hands into my front pockets and headed back to my dorm room.

With a steaming cup of Ramen Noodles for sustenance and a Mountain Dew for focus, I sprawled on my bed with notebooks and textbooks alike strewn around my laptop. Alternating between slurping and sipping, I found that I had reread the same section of my psychology textbook three times. I sighed scrubbing my eyes with the soles of my hands in hopes of stimulating concentration. Every other thought I had was about her, and every time I blinked I saw her face, a knowing smirk carefully tucked in the corner of her mouth.

After several hours of pushing the boulder up the mountain, I finished the last of my homework. Slamming the numerous text books shut with a satisfying "crack," I *stacked them haphazardly and set them on my desk. Then the waiting began. And so did the interior monologue.*

She probably felt sorry for me, I thought, that's why she offered to help. Anything she felt for me is completely platonic and nothing is ever going to come of this. But maybe she liked the quiet sensitive types. Maybe there's a little bit of hope. But who could love someone who was so obviously damaged goods? How would she react if she found out how my heart had broken? Would she leave me the same way he had? I didn't think I could recover from another blow like that.

The seconds felt like minutes. My mind asked questions and answered them in the most negative manner it could manage. My heart decided it wanted to run a marathon without me, and the moment my head hit my pillow the adrenaline flooded my veins. I tried everything from warm milk to meditation but nothing could quiet the excitement flowing through me.

A steady rain had settled over the campus during the few seconds of sleep I managed to catch and I tugged on a beanie in lieu of using a hairbrush. I had a brief but searing hot fling with a Styrofoam cup of bitter coffee and felt slightly more human as I slogged through my Friday morning classes. In a sprint from one side of the quad to another, I caught sight of the rain goddess Morgan who was soaked to the bone and shivering in yellow rain boots. She grinned at me and I waved awkwardly before flinging myself at the half open door to my Creative Writing class.

Kicking off my soggy shoes at the door, I padded across the atrocious blue and red acrylic carpet to my spot in the circle. I took my place between the quiet but deep brunette and the pretentious blonde who was convinced he was the next Shakespeare. There was nothing I needed more than to pour my soul onto paper in the form of ink and the moment the prompt was suggested I ran with it. Twisting my essence into something desirable, I filled the page with who I wanted to be, who Morgan wanted.

The grin on my face was undeniable but it fell as the words were said out loud. The realization that I could never fulfill all the expectations the world and I had for myself was soul-sucking. Thunder rumbled overhead echoing the sound my heart made. I packed all my pages haphazardly into my notebook and hugged it to my chest as I made my way back to my dorm in the drizzling rain.

A gust of wind tugged at the messy corners and freed one of the papers. Against all odds it sailed across the quad and splayed itself across Morgan's perfect lips. Laughing she peeled it off and walked over to me, eyes skimming across the page. I froze. My thinly veiled metaphor was in her hands and I knew any chance I had with her was shot. She took the notebook from my grasp and tucked the sheet safely inside.

"You're a good writer, but I don't like these characters. Ren thinks so highly of Margie and tries so hard to impress her that she doesn't see that Margie is in love with her, too," Morgan explained, a small smile pulling at her lips.

"How do you know Ren is a girl? It never says," I asked defensively.

"You told the story as Ren, but I know Margie's perspective and she likes Ren just the way she is," she said taking a step forward.

Her fingers entwined in my hair and pulled my lips to hers. The kiss tasted like salt not from her ocean but from mine as it poured from my eyes and down my cheeks but she didn't seem to mind. It was all so new and beautiful. There were no hard angles or rough stubble only soft, smooth skin and full, wanton lips. Pulling away, she laughed, eyes focused on something behind me and I turned my head to see the sun beaming through the clouds refracting off raindrops in a perfect arc. I laughed too, tears still streaming down my face before I caught her mouth with mine feeling her grin against my own.

"We're still on for that study date, right?" Morgan asked using her thumbs to brush stray tears and raindrops from my cheeks. Her teasing smile was all I had ever wanted so of course I nodded my head and kissed her again.

"Sounds good." I grinned.

Vocabulary

Define the following and add any new words that you have encountered recently:

Obtrusive

Plausible

Writing Prompts

1. The Argument -- Recall a conflict you've recently had with someone. What happened? How did you feel? Now write about the conflict as if you were the other person.

2. Look at a picture that stimulates or excites your imagination for about five minutes. Think about the scenery and the people. Who are they, what are they doing, why? How did they get there, where are they going? What are they worried about? What are their problems? Now write. Don't try to edit. Give them a situation and see what happens.

Chapter Eighteen
Writing the Short Prose Piece

Often you will not be able to articulate your theme, or what your story is about, until you have written a first draft. Give yourself permission in that first draft not to get it right. It may be that you know exactly what happens next and next and next. Great. Keep writing. Even if you don't, keep writing.

Don't worry about the descriptions or the metaphors or even your spelling—especially your spelling in your first draft. In fact, I suggest that you turn off your spellcheck and your grammar check. Wait until you are completely done with the piece and then do a spell check. But spell cheek never replaces a good eyeball proofing because, as you can see, a misspelled word may correctly spell another word.

Choosing Point of View

One of the most important choices you will make about your story is point of view. A lot of fiction written these days is either in the first person or the close third person. Close third person is similar to first person because the character's sensibility is the lens through which we perceive the events of the story. First person and close third person give the writer a tremendous advantage -- we get to know everything that the character sees, hears, thinks and feels. We are privy to the character's internal monologue. Sometimes I think this is one of the main reasons we read: we want to get in someone else's head and find out what that is like.

But some writers don't take full advantage of first person or close third person. They underutilize that wonderful device we call point of view. Here's the thing: if you are going to use a close third person or a first person point of view, you need to spend some time in that character's head. What is the character thinking? Or not thinking!

Why is it important? Mainly, it helps your reader identify with the character, care about the character, and understand the character's motivations. When you withhold information that a point of view character should know because you don't want to give everything away, you run the risk of making your reader feel cheated.

The more we get in your head or your character's, the more engaged we will be in your story.

There are other types of point of view: omniscient, limited omniscient, and so on. However, for the purposes of this lesson, I suggest you choose either a first person narrator or a close third-person point of view.

Example of first person narrator:

I walked to the store with my little brother. He was always wanting to go with me everywhere. I tried to sneak off sometimes by myself, but every time I turned around, there he was like my shadow.

Example of close-third person narrator:

Tyler reluctantly took his little brother to the store. Mikey insisted on going everywhere that Tyler went, but Tyler wished he could just be alone sometimes. Once in a while, Tyler would sneak out the back door and head through the woods to his secret hideout, but as soon as he looked around, he'd see Mikey following him just like a shadow. Go away, he'd think. But it wouldn't do any good.

Using Metaphors and Symbols to Convey Theme

The quality that makes prose narrative "art" is the selection of images and the subtle utilization of symbols to create an emotional impact on the reader.

The types of metaphors you use in your story will serve as a thematic indication to the reader. Metaphors often become symbols that help convey the main idea of the story. For example, if you begin a story by comparing something to "an open wound," then your reader will want to know what wounds this story is going to be about. In her book *Tar Baby*, Toni Morrison includes a scene with butterflies congregating about the character's window. It is a perfect symbol for the character's sexual awakening, and no doubt the author knew this.

Many times writers use symbols and metaphors unconsciously in the first draft. By examining the metaphors you use unconsciously, you can start weeding out the ones that don't contribute to the meaning of the story and using more of those that do.

Imagery and symbol are intertwined. A creative writer must carefully choose the images that will contribute to the effect she is trying to create. Is the tree outside her window in full leaf the right image? What does a tree in full leaf convey to the reader? Fullness of life? Fecundity? Does the writer choose images that will underscore the meaning of his story or those that serve to comment on the events in the story by offering contrast?

Look closely at a story that you find especially moving or interesting. What are the images that the writer chooses to include? Remember, life is full of irrelevant, incidental images. The writer's art is the selection of images to lead the reader to some sort of insight.

The following passages are excerpts from a work-in-progress by writer Rebecca Wallace-Aktas. Notice the selection of images. Now, not every single image is going to be a conscious choice on the part of the writer. Sometimes, the selection is unconscious, but as the story goes through revisions, making decisions about what images to keep and which to discard becomes a conscious process separating the wheat from the chaff in order to create a unified sense of meaning or purpose. In the first excerpt, the narrator has gone to her mother's home for Thanksgiving. Her mother is ill, but they have gone shopping anyway:

> I pull the grocery list from my pocket and search for a pen; I cannot find one. Mom begins pushing the cart, as if to tour the outer rim of the grocery store. She doesn't stop. I realize this as I collect waxy, yellow, red and green peppers and see Mom gradually moving through the bulk, dried food section.

These images have connotative value. The narrator is collecting food that is alive and healthy while her mother leaves her behind and moves through the "dried food" section—the food that has been drained of life. Later the mother's illness worsens and she has to go to the hospital:

> Mom climbs in her bed; the bed has been turned down for her as if she is being tucked in for a night's sleep. It is as if she is home, and she is; this is her realm. She spent 30 years here as a nurse, a healer. She knows the lingo. She can read the charts and the body language. Evan and I leave Mother here with her husband and her friends and we go to the waiting area. This room is of light pastels, salmon-colored walls, worn chairs and a couch. A fish tank is in the corner, at an angle.

This brief description conveys an atmosphere of the surreal. The light-colored walls are meant to be cheerful, but the effect of the worn chairs and couch is drab and depressing. The fish in the tank are alive, but they are in a "tank." The mother is alive but she is also in an artificial situation. I like the little addition of "at an angle." It conveys the sense that something isn't right. Then the narrator returns to the hospital room and provides a succinct description of the mother:

> I look at Mom, her eyes are puffy; does the Doctor not see that her eyes are puffy? Mom's little feet are crossed, with her bright white tennis shoes on. The bottoms, the soles, are as clean as a whistle, no wear.

One detail is all that is necessary to show the narrator's concern: the mother's eyes are puffy. Something is wrong. And then this image is juxtaposed with the image of the clean soles of the "bright white tennis shoes." The contrast of the illness in the puffy eyes and the clean bright shoes conveys so much heartbreak, not to mention the "little feet" that heighten the sense of the mother's vulnerability.

It's a balancing act, and that's what makes writing fiction an art. Your use of symbols should be natural and not forced, and they should be individualized for your character's particular situation. Don't use snakes to represent "evil" unless a snake would naturally be a part of the character's world. Find the images and symbols that are particular to the situation and yet can still be universalized to create a wider meaning.

Story Writing Guidelines

The following are guidelines. They are not rules, but if you follow them you'll find your writing is generally more accessible and more interesting and will more effectively get your point across.

- Choose one main character. As soon as your reader begins reading your story, he or she is casting about for someone to take them on the ride. Let us know from sentence one who that main character is. In other words, if Spike is your main character, don't start the story with Danielle wondering what she is going to do that night. This is Spike's story. Spike is the guy your reader is supposed to care about.

- For shorter pieces (anything that isn't novel length), it's a good idea to keep us in that main character's head. Let us see what he sees, feel what he feels and hear his thoughts. Don't go into another character's head unless it's absolutely necessary. So many times a writer will switch from one point of view to another (or from one character's head to another) when we don't need to know what that other character is thinking.

- If you need to show what another character is thinking, do it through dialogue or through action. If, for some greater artistic purpose, you want to change to another character's point of view and spend some time in their heads, then put in a space break and make it clear to the reader that you have changed point of view. But always ask yourself: is this necessary to the story? Sometimes it is, but if you do it too often, your reader doesn't know whom to care about.

- Stories are not real life. They are both more and less than real life. Good writers are selective about what they put in their stories, and they are merciless about killing anything that does not serve the story. In general, one of two things happens in the story. Through a series of (often unfortunate) events, the main character changes in some way. She grows, she learns something, she understands life in a way she hadn't understood it before. OR through this series of events, something important is revealed to the reader, and it is the reader who learns something, who grows or who is changed. CHANGE is the key.

- Try to "show" as much as you can. Create scenes and imagine that you are a movie camera; help your reader to see, hear, touch and smell the events you describe. But make sure each scene furthers the aims of the story. Avoid having a scene just for the sake of having a scene, or dialogue for the sake of dialogue. When your characters are talking, make sure what they say is relevant to the story. If it isn't, then make use of your delete button.

- Keep descriptions of the dialog simple. It's okay to sometimes add things like "in an angry tone" but generally the reader should be able to figure out by the dialogue itself.

- The shorter the period of time you try to cover, the better you can develop your scenes.
- Keep your verb tenses consistent. Most people write in the past tense, but some write in the present tense. In some stories, the narration is given in the past tense while the character's direct thoughts are in the present tense. That's okay because his thoughts would be in the present tense at the time.
- Ask yourself: what am I trying to show through this story? What is the point of this story? What would I like my reader to come away with after reading this story? Imagine that your reader is a complete stranger to the world you are describing. Would he or she understand something about that world they hadn't before?

Writing Assignment:

Finish your narrative prose piece. Go over it and add in the images (metaphors and symbols) that will underscore your theme.

Student Writing Sample

Darker than Normal

by Grady Garrison

Sitting in the sterile hallway, the smell of disinfectant tinged with decay blocking out almost all other sensory perception, I stare blankly at the wall across from me. This place is buzzing almost as if it was its own small city, even though it's 2:30 in the morning. White-robed doctors stroll past, leisurely walking and staring at charts as if they were more interested in numbers and diagrams than in the disturbingly ill and pain-saturated people they were going to see. Nurses clad in those sickening green scrubs rocket past with a never-ending sense of urgency. The place is so pristine that it's always a slight shock when one of those usually immaculate green garments walks out of a room covered in a darker-than-normal shade of crimson.

I begin to get selfishly annoyed at all the activity and noise. I've been sitting here for the last 15 minutes, trying to reflect on the events of the evening. Focusing on what I deem to be an educational, life-changing moment proves difficult, however, with the sound of phones ringing, voices over the P.A. system, carts being wheeled back and forth and, of course, the occasional anguish-filled screams coming from a room down the hall. Electing to withdraw myself from that organized chaos, I retreat to the room into which I was afraid to venture not 30 minutes ago.

The room, like all others in the emergency room, is a bland shade of blue, which serves the purpose of neither eliciting any kind of emotional response, nor drawing attention to the pathetic, limp figure on the cardboard-like sheets in the midst of all the computers, tubes and wires. A short time ago, six or seven people surrounded this bed, offering comfort, expressing relief and, occasionally, shooting angry glances. Now, however, they appear to have vacated the area, if only temporarily; perhaps they're getting snacks from the waiting room.

Taking solace in the brief reprieve, I grab a Spartan chair sitting next to a small table in the corner of the room and pull it up to the bed. I settle myself into the chair, not without a fair amount of discomfort, and once again survey the damage I caused. Angela lies there, unconscious and peaceful now, though before she was awake and stoically fighting the pain that must surely have been careening up and down her spine. I grab her hand, careful not to disturb her rest, and sit there a moment, eyes closed, breathing in the disinfected air. Finally, I have time to consider what happened tonight.

* * *

Out of the corner of my eyes I can see John leaning out the front passenger window, and a small part of me, in the back of my mind, thinks I should probably yell at him to sit back down.

Instead, with one hand on the wheel, I take my right fist and bash him as hard as I can in the thigh.

"Ah! What the hell?" he yells in pain and retreats back into the vehicle.

Chuckling to myself, I return my attention to the road and turn up the music. John, next to me, switches to a track we all love and have completely overplayed in the past month. I look into the rearview mirror to be sure the other car is still following us, and even though all I can see is their headlights, I know it's them. We were all a little disappointed we didn't make it to the haunted house, yet we still managed to make a good time of it. That's how we were. Anything we did, whether it was classwork, amusement parks, paintball wars or simply lounging about the house, we made it more fun that it should have been. Combining this innovative, creative spirit with my newly acquired drivers' license opened up endless opportunities to us.

Of course, now that we had these opportunities, we naturally made no attempt to take advantage of them. We spent about a month driving around our hometown in the dark green Saturn my grandmother had given me, blasting music, looking at girls and feeling pretty damn cool. Finally, however, near the beginning of October, we decided to spread our wings a little bit. I printed out directions to a haunted house located about 20 miles from home and off we went.

"I can't believe you got us lost," John says for about the ninth time.

"Seriously man, I didn't get us lost. It's not my fault if MapQuest gives me bad directions," I explain.

After the half hour drive to the haunted house's supposed location, it was nowhere to be found. We drove around a seemingly random neighborhood, looking to all the world like criminals, I'm sure, for about 20 minutes before deciding to pack it up and go home.

Now, driving back, John, Mandy and Angie with me in my car, and Andrew, Rob and Alex in the car behind us, we find ourselves up to our old tricks, making the best of a bad situation. I roll down both back windows because I know the girls hate the cold, damp air of a rainy October night and because being ornery is in my nature. Right at that moment, the light shifts in my eyes and I hear the rush of a large object flying past my side of the car, while the sharp, staccato sound of a blaring horn informs us that our companions in the rear car think they are so much cooler than us.

I look forward, watching their taillights getting smaller, much quicker than they should, before I glance at John.

"Go get 'em." He doesn't even hesitate.

I nod and, without saying a word, floor it. An idiotic grin spreads across my face as, for the first time, I feel the adrenaline that driving a two-ton killing machine at reckless speeds can bring. The girls are screaming in the back seat, but it's that fake, forced scream one might hear on a roller coaster or at a boy band concert – or like the ones we were hoping to hear at that damn haunted house.

As the pavement and streetlights fly past us faster and faster, it begins to feel like we're going a little too fast. John is still egging me on from the front seat, but I look down at the speedometer, which has rotated clockwise the fastest I've ever seen it – 113 miles per hour! Grandma would be proud!

Now, I know we're moving too fast, and even though the taillights we were chasing are still ahead of us, I remove my foot from the gas pedal. As soon as he feels the car decelerating, even John intones, "uh, you may want to slow down we've got a curve coming up."

I see the curve coming, but I'm afraid to hit the brake because I don't know what slowing down that quickly would do to a car going this fast. To the right of the curve is a grass expanse followed by an on-ramp from the bridge we're passing under. I glance back down at the speedometer, (103 mph) and, when I look up again, the curve is upon us. To me, it seems to arrive faster than physically possible.

I turn the steering wheel a bit too far.

Suddenly, there is a faint splash, so faint the others may not have even heard it, but it was enough to make the car begin to slide. Panicked now, my hands jerking the steering wheel hard to the right are not only fighting the uncontrollable skid, but also the creeping desperation trying to take control. The car swings out of the skid, but I've turned far too much. The car slips across the entire road and out onto the median, where I once again yank the steering wheel as hard as I can, this time to the right, trying to avoid a crash.

Success! We're out of the median and back onto the road, but still going way too fast, and I still don't have control of the car. We're now skidding, parallel to the on-ramp, across the road, off the road, onto the wet grass, and finally it happens.

For a brief moment, eternity fills the span of a single second. As both the front and back tires on the right side of my car strike the lip of the on-ramp simultaneously, time stops. Apart from one brief, strangled scream from the back seat – I'm not sure if it's Angie or Mandy – and the gasp we all issue as our collective breath is suspended, there is absolute silence. My life does not flash before my eyes, there is no light at the end of any tunnel, but here I am having cohesive thoughts as my car hurtles through the air. I think, Oh my god. We're flying through the air. We've now completed one flip and are still in the air. Did something just hit the car? That was loud. Is this ever going to end?

And then it does. The car comes to a stop, and disorientation reigns. As I'm trying to discern my surroundings, I hear John's unnerved voice: "Is everyone alright?" That's when I hear crying and gasping from the backseat. I'm still trying to get my bearings. It's too dark to see anything so everything has to be done through sound and feel. I can hardly breath, so I undo my seatbelt, and my legs, which had been dangling, fall to the floor. How did John get on my left side? That's when I realize that the car finally came to rest on its roof.

"I can't get my door open," John says.

Hesitantly, I try mine. Same result. The doors are jammed, and the windows won't roll down. Panic is truly setting in now and, without saying a word to each other, John and I both begin to kick frantically at the windshield. I hear it crack, but it doesn't budge. I elbow the driver-side window, which is now on my right, as hard as I can, but it too resists. Somewhere in the back of my mind I realize that striking something that hard should probably have hurt, but I felt nothing. I try again, and finally I hear the immensely relieving and satisfying shattering of the glass.

When I crawl out of the car, shaken and terrified, it takes me a moment to get to my feet. My entire body is quaking and seems intent to punish me by refusing to do as I command. I look up from my position and see that a semi has pulled over near us, and the driver is sprinting towards us. As I finally get to my feet, John and Mandy both crawl out of the car, though Mandy made her way through the gaping hole where the back door used to be. The only person we're missing is Angie.

The truck driver, who had been speaking to someone, presumably 911, on his cell phone, hangs it up and looks at me.

"You're bleeding pretty bad man." He's pointing at my elbow.

I glance down at it, and sure enough, my entire right sleeve below the elbow has turned red. I pluck at the sleeve, still not feeling any pain, and see the holes the shards of glass cut into it.

In a dazed wonder, I extricate myself from the company of the benevolent stranger, seeking to make sense of the chaos that just broached our lives. Turning around, I look at the wreckage. The scene that greets me is like something out of a war movie. John and Mandy are attempting to pull an unconscious figure from beneath the wreckage of the overturned car. It appears Angie struck her head on the roof of the car after unbuckling her seat belt, rendering her unconscious. As my other senses begin returning, I notice the gaping hole where the engine used to be is smoking and a pungent smell of gasoline has enveloped the entire area.

The truck driver rushes past me to help John and Mandy. My ears have been ringing ever since leaving the car, so I can't make out what he's saying, but my eyes follow his frantically pointing finger about 30 yards away to the gas tank that was ripped from the car, its contents now voided onto the grassy area we currently occupy. As soon as my slowly moving brain comprehends the situation, I run to the aid of the trio, and the four of us finally pull Angie from the smoldering wreckage and make our way up to the on-ramp, where we sit weeping uncontrollably while waiting for our ride to the hospital.

It's astonishing that the moment life becomes the most real, the most tangible, is the same moment you see people in fear for their lives. Shutting my eyes, I try to block out the sobbing coming from my friends, the shouting coming from the truck driver and the wailing coming from the approaching sirens.

* * *

My eyes open, and the first thing I see is a blinking green light. Immediately a wave of relief floods over me as I realize that the reality of 30 seconds ago is in fact a farce; a concocted memory meant to trick my mind into believing what's not real. I close my eyes again, reveling in the feeling when finally my other senses kick in. When I hear a rhythmic, high-pitched beeping coinciding with the flashing green light, I take another look around. It's then that I notice I physically can't take a look around, as my neck is immobilized and I have tubes shooting into my veins. I see people standing around me; my fingers grasp the cardboard-like sheets under my hands and finally reality confronts my dream-addled brain. The accident hospitalized me. I'm here, alive, but everyone looks so terribly sad. That's because I'm here, barely alive, and I'm the only one.

Vocabulary

Define the following and add any new words you have found:

Articulate (verb)

Fecundity

Juxtapose

Omniscient

Succinct

Conclusion

Chapter Nineteen
The Writing Workshop

A writing workshop is a place where writers get together to critique each other's work. It is often done in an academic environment. But you can form a workshop with other writers and meet at a coffee shop or at someone's house or you can join a workshop online.

Workshops can be extremely useful if they are conducted the right way. But sometimes the criticism is not constructive. And sometimes other writers will try to rewrite your poem, story or play for you.

To avoid these pitfalls, try to establish a workshop where the emphasis is on questions. Which do you think is a more productive response—"I hate the way this story ends" or "How am I supposed to feel at the end of this story (poem/play)?" Our job in a workshop is to help the writer understand what is missing. Many times the writer knows the material so well that he or she forgets what the reader doesn't know. It is our job as fellow writers to let her know by asking detailed questions about what we can't see, hear, smell or feel—and more importantly to let the writer know what piques our curiosity.

Effective Workshops

Even if you are a student in the workshop, you can guide the tone of the workshop by following these steps yourself and by asking your readers what questions they had as they read your work.

Here's how I run my workshops:

First, participants identify what they believe the story is about. They may also discuss how they personally related to incidents in the story. This is important because it can help the writer identify her audience.

Secondly, participants point out the strengths of the piece (e.g. structure, dialogue, characterization, conflict, use of language). On the actual typescript they might put check marks by sentences, phrases or words which are especially strong or powerful. The writer needs to know the strengths of the piece in order to develop them and not lose them in the revision process. It's a wonderful feeling to see all those check marks dotting the margins. The checkmarks are the proverbial spoonful of sugar, sweetening the more critical comments.

Finally, the participants begin to ask questions. These questions are not to be answered by the writer during the workshop. The writer takes these questions home, mulls over them and then decides which ones, if any, she will choose to answer in the text. The writer's peers cannot write his story for him. Ultimately, the responsibility must go back to the writer.

There are three general types of questions that are useful in workshops:

- Big Picture Questions. What's at stake in the story? What is the point of the story? How am I supposed to feel about these characters? Is this the best structure for the story? What if it was told as a flashback? Whose story is it? What is the motivation for this character?

- Logistical/Technical Questions. These questions address any confusion in the reader's mind. How did that happen? Where was the character standing when that took place? Do you really want to switch point of view? What does that add? Is that middle section necessary? What is the significance of a certain event?

- Detail Questions. These questions help the writer identify where he needs to add details to create a sense of "thereness." What kind of shoes was the character wearing? What does it smell like in that hospital room? What did her face look like when she found out the secret? What was going on in the body? These questions can be silly and seem unimportant. That's fine. Asking them helps the writer to generate the rich sensory details that make a story come alive. Ultimately, it is always the writer's choice whether or not to answer these questions. The kind of shoes may be completely unimportant. Or it may be that the character's red stiletto heels with his business suit tell us something important about who he is.

There are no assignments or vocabulary words for this chapter.

Chapter Twenty
Seeing it Again: Revision

In an interview in the 1956 issue of the *The Paris Review*, Ernest Hemingway had the following conversation:

> *Interviewer: How much rewriting do you do?*

> *Hemingway: It depends. I rewrote the ending of Farewell to Arms, the last page of it, 39 times before I was satisfied.*

> *Interviewer: Was there some technical problem there? What was it that had stumped you?*

> *Hemingway: Getting the words right.*

Revision means to "see again." Revision is more than just going through your work and adding or subtracting commas. Real revision entails looking at your work as if it were not your own and seeing what needs to be done to make it as strong as it can be. Sometimes that means a complete rewrite, starting at a new point in the story, or finding the perfect ending. It might mean changing the point of view or changing from past tense to present. There are so many variables.

Steps for revision:

- Put the piece of writing aside for a while and work on something else. Leave it alone for at least a week.
- Now reread it and ask yourself where it seems to stall, and where you've gotten distracted from what you were trying to say. If it's a poem, are there words that are stale or inaccurate?
- Get feedback. If you have a writing group or are taking a class in creative writing, that is ideal. A writing group consists of three or more other writers, whose opinions you trust. These writers might be classmates or you might be in an online writing group. You might also get feedback from a creative writing teacher or an editor.
- If possible get someone to read the piece aloud to you. Or you can read it out loud yourself. Reading aloud helps you hear the sound of your work. If something isn't working, you're more likely to hear it than you are to see it.

- Think about the feedback you've received. Sometimes it might seem that other people just "don't get it." You may be right, but it is always worth considering their feedback. It is up to you whether or not to make changes to your work.
- Make the revisions that seem right to you. Now put it aside again.
- Reread the work. If you think it's as good as it's going to get for now, then go through and do a final polish. Make sure every word is the right word. Check your grammar and spelling, and then you're good to go. Chances are you might have to go back to step one and start all over again. If so, try not to get frustrated. Writing can be a long process.

Revising Poetry

Poets may take years to write one poem. If you are in a class, you don't have years, but you do have a chance to look over your poems and decide how you can make them better.

Look at your line breaks and punctuation. Would changing them make the poem better? What about the stanzas? Can you rearrange them? Do you want to add another stanza? Or cut one? Read each word. Is it the best word you can use? Where can you cut words and still express your meaning? Finally, consider your title. Is it evocative? Is there a better title?

Revising Dramatic Scenes

Once you've heard your scenes read aloud, you will probably notice lines that sounded flat or places where the story was unclear. You will want to go over the dialogue carefully. Are there lines that don't add anything to the story or that don't propel the plot forward? Do the characters speak in a way that is individualized and interesting? Do the lines help us understand who the characters are and what they care about?

Next look at your premise. Is it clear? Is it the best premise for these characters? Ask yourself whether your characters ring true. Are they believable? What makes the audience care about them?

Finally, look at the action of the play. Is there a clear motivation for the things that the characters do? Is there enough action? Or too much?

Revising Narrative Prose

Once you've written the first draft of your story, you will begin to understand what it is you are trying to say. Why did this incident or this series of events inspire you to share the story? Some people may know even before they write the first word of a story what its purpose is, but many of us are not always sure what it is that compels us to write about a particular subject. Something—an image, a place, a phrase—haunts us and so we write about it.

As you go through your piece, eliminate anything that doesn't contribute to the meaning of the story. You don't need to keep something just because "it happened that way." Pay attention to point of view. Do you accidentally slip into the thoughts of a character that is not your main point of view character? Are you giving your readers enough interior monologue for them to understand and care about your main character?

As with drama, you must look at dialogue and make sure it serves a purpose. You will also want to make sure that each image adds to a unified whole. And as with poetry, you will want to look at each word and decide if there is a better, fresher way to say what you want to say.

Assignment:

Revise your work to turn in to your class or to submit to a publisher. It may be a selection of poetry, your short play, or your prose narrative. Make significant changes to your work. Then go through it carefully and make sure your spelling and grammar are correct (except in those cases in which you intentionally are writing in vernacular).

Student Writing Sample

This story by student writer Casey Wiginton came from a prompt he was given to write a story about an abandoned miniature golf course. Notice how he writes from a female point of view. The story does not have a resolution and yet it manages to evoke powerful emotions in the reader. A neatly packaged resolution is not always necessary. Sometimes a powerful image at the end tells us everything we need to know.

What's Already Here

by Casey Wiginton

We walk together without saying anything and the heat makes us sweat and the dust from the grass turns to mud against my shins, but it's fine. All I'm worried about is whether or not this flask has enough to get me drunk. I look back at Daniel to make sure he's keeping up. He didn't expect my sense of adventure.

We cuss and stagger through the thicket as bugs and things get in my face and hair and I use my hands to cut a way out and we push into the clearing and it's an old parking lot and he takes my hand and I let him guide me even though I could do it with my eyes shut.

When we get to the fence, I throw my purse over and Daniel hoists me up and I wonder if I look stupid when I land and he lands next to me and everything burns when I think about it. Nothing fixes this. Warm vodka and lemonade runs down my chin as I swig with my stupid desperation. My neck gets sticky.

Under the cicada's prayer, I can hear the rusty batting cages bang open and shut. I walk through the mini-golf course, hoping there are ghosts. I hope there are things hiding and waiting to slaughter us. I'm more afraid of what's already here. I clutch my stomach. There are dull, hidden pains inside of me and they're not getting any duller. As we walk past each hole, I run my fingers along the toad king or the magical castle guarding them -- everything steamy and sun bleached. Daniel tries to tell me things about this place like I didn't grow up having all my birthday parties here. But I let him talk. I think about how maybe if I get drunk every day I'll eventually kill the life that's forming and pee it out like Becky did. It comes out like strings, she said, like a bunch of bloody spaghetti.

We come to the windmill and he pries open a little door along the side and I drop down and crawl into the hidden spaces. It's dark and cool inside and there's an old motor that used to spin the blades and I stick my fingers in and grab a handful of cobwebs and laugh as Daniel squirms away from me.

This was always the hardest hole, the last stop where the ball drops down a tunnel and rolls back to the beginning. I reach for Daniel through the dark and lie and let him think we'll be okay. The right words are too hard to find. He believes me and I believe myself. It isn't there. He cracks his knuckles against my chest and drinks the vodka from my skin. The truth is only made of broken windmills. Daniel is strong and I am stronger. I reach my hand into the darkness for another handful of cobwebs and squeeze as hard as I can.

Resources

Abercrombie, Barbara. *A Year of Writing Dangerously*. Novato, California: New World Library. 2012.

Bishop, Wendy. *Working Words: The Process of Creative Writing*. Mountain View, CA: Mayfield Publishing. 1992.

Brown, Rita Mae. *Starting From Scratch: A Different Kind of Writer's Manual*. New York: Bantam. 1989

Burroway, Janet. *Writing Fiction: A Guide to Narrative Craft*, Sixth Edition. Boston: Addison Wesley Longman. 2002

Dillard, Annie. *The Writing Life, Pilgrim at Tinker Creek, An American Childhood*. New York: Quality Paperback Book Club. 1990

Gerard, Philip and Carolyn Forche. W*riting Creative Nonfiction: Instruction Insights from Teachers of the Associated Writing Programs*. Cincinnati: Writer's Digest Books. 2001

Goldberg, Natalie. *Writing Down the Bones* and *Wild Mind*. New York: Quality Paperback Book Club. 1990

Gutkind, Lee. *The Art of Creative Nonfiction: Writing and Selling the Literature of Reality*. New York: John Wiley & Sons. 1997

Hills, Rust. *Writing in General and the Short Story in Particular*. Revised Ed. Boston: Houghton Mifflin Co. 1987

Lamott, Anne. *Bird by Bird: Some Instructions on Writing and Life*. New York: Pantheon Books. 1994

Novakovitch, Josip. *Fiction Writer's Workshop*. Cincinnati: Story Press. 1995

Novakovitch, Josip. *Writing Fiction Step by Step*. Cincinnati: Story Press. 1998

Pollack, Eileen. "The Interplay of Form and Content in Creative Nonfiction." *The Writer's Chronicle*. Fairfax, VA. March/April, 2007.

Sellers, Heather. *Page After Page: Discover the confidence and passion you need to start writing and keep writing (no matter what)*. Cincinnati: Writer's Digest Books. 2005

Schneider, Pat. *Writing Alone and With Others*. Oxford University Press, 2003, and available at www.patschneider.com.

Stern, Jerome. *Making Shapely Fiction*. Paperback. New York: Norton. 2000

Stern, Jerome. *Radios: Short Takes on Life and Culture*. Norton: 1997

About the Author

Pat MacEnulty holds a doctorate from the creative writing program at the Florida State University. Her novels include *Sweet Fire*, *Time to Say Goodbye*, *Picara*, and *From May to December*. She is also the author of the short story collection *The Language of Sharks*, the memoir *Wait Until Tomorrow*, and a Shakespeare adaptation for children entitled *Puck and the Mushy Gushy Love Potion*. She has been delivering creative writing workshops in a variety of venues since 1995. She is an Associate Professor of English at Johnson & Wales University in Charlotte, North Carolina, where she teaches creative writing, film, journalism, and composition.